IN THE FIELD

IN THE FIELD

A Real-Life Survival Guide for the Social Work Internship

WILLIAM A. DANOWSKI

Dominican College

Boston   New York   San Francisco
Mexico City   Montreal   Toronto   London   Madrid   Munich   Paris
Hong Kong   Singapore   Tokyo   Cape Town   Sydney

Series Editor: *Patricia Quinlin*
Editorial Assistant: *Annemarie Kennedy*
Marketing Manager: *Kris Ellis-Levy*
Editorial Production Service: *Chestnut Hill Enterprises, Inc.*
Manufacturing Buyer: *JoAnne Sweeney*
Cover Administrator: *Rebecca Krzyzaniak*
Electronic Composition: *Omegatype Typography, Inc.*

For related titles and support materials, visit our online catalog at
www.ablongman.com

Between the time Website information is gathered and then published, some sites
may have closed. Also, the transcription of URLs can result in typographical errors.
The publisher would appreciate being notified of any problems with URLs so that
they may be corrected in subsequent editions.

Library of Congress Cataloging-in-Publication Data

Danowski, William A.
  In the field : a real-life survival guide for the social work intern / William A.
Danowski.
     p. cm.
  Includes bibliographical references and index.
  ISBN 0-205-37600-2
  1. Social work education. 2. Internship programs. I. Title.

HV11.D357 2005
361.3'071'55–dc22

                                                            2004016581

Printed in the United States of America
10   9   8   7   6   5   09   08   07

To past, present, and future social-work students:
May you serve joyfully and well.

CONTENTS

■ ■ ■ ■ ■

CHAPTER THREE
Beginning at the Beginning   29

CHAPTER FOUR
Staying the Course   47

CHAPTER FIVE

Navigating the Hazards   73

CHAPTER SIX

Termination   91

INTRODUCTION

I am writing this book because of a student who announced one day, "I need a how-to book." It's a natural request, but writing a simple guide book to a complex set of experiences such as the social work internship is much easier said than done.

In the Field is a practical, down-to-earth, practice-based book, not a collection of theories. The purpose of this book is to help you move from the world of the classroom, textbook, and theory to the real world of practice, where you will begin to apply the theories you have already learned.

If you feel nervous, inadequate to the task, or unprepared, welcome to the club. If you're certain you haven't learned all the right theories or haven't learned them well enough, that's a natural feeling. And if you're sure you don't know enough, this book is for you. This handbook is designed to show you how you will learn by doing, no matter your starting point. It will show you how to let coworkers, supervisors, and life itself teach you so you will begin to trust your inner wisdom.

Caution: This book is not a book of quick fixes or a book of easy solutions to complex problems. It is a guide to help you prepare for and enter your social-work field placement with some general ideas and orientations that will help you begin a rewarding and successful career.

I have been a social work supervisor for over twenty-five years, and have mentored countless interns. I have used this experience to write a book that presents examples from real situations, people, and events. I have also included feedback from former students who have completed their first field placement and lived to tell about it. I have invited you, the reader, into supervision sessions with students in order to get the behind-the-scenes coaching about the competing political agendas you may need to be aware of. The scenarios in the book are all taken from actual client situations and student encounters. The names of the clients have been changed for the purpose of confidentiality, and the same is true for the student material presented.

As you read the examples of difficulties encountered or see mistakes other students have made, please don't snicker or say "I would never do that. How stupid!" You will learn that these situations are common and that, going into a new and unknown environment, almost every student will make embarrassing missteps and will experience similar learning situations.

In the conceptual phase of writing this book, I used two instrumental metaphors: The first was to think of an internship as a tool box to which you will add tools as you learn. Each new skill learned is an addition to the chest of tools. The second was to conceive of a social work internship as a sea voyage, as a journey for which you are preparing, one filled with potential and predictable hazards that you must be on the alert for.

Social work students are on a voyage, and they are filling a chest with tools. Students might take their skills and what they need to learn to become a social worker for granted. Thus, your internship is helping you fill the chest with tools to do the job, tools that you should treasure. They are new skills and attitudes that are essential to your place in the world as a professional social worker.

You will encounter a number of other metaphors in this book. Some of them conceptualize ways you will work with your clients and how you will come to understand abstract concepts. You will also learn to be on the alert for metaphors your clients use, and how to use these as vital elements in your work with your clients.

ACKNOWLEDGMENTS

I would like to thank the many individuals who, as students or interns, have made *In the Field* possible—in particular, those who shared their experiences and provided feedback on my ideas and drafts: Leroy Ennis, Nicole Madonna, Dana Scalora, and MaryLynn Schiller.

Grateful thanks are due to Ellen Moore and Christopher Tavella, who spent countless hours editing my drafts. Without their efforts this book would have remained an idea unwritten. Ellen's encouragement during the early stages of the book clearly helped transform the ramblings of a social worker supervisor into a book. Every book needs a finisher and clearly Chris was the man for this task. Like building a home, I had the good fortune to have a great crew to write this book. I am indebted to Chris for his contributions to the content, making the finished product a better book.

I want to thank the following reviewers for their kind remarks and helpful suggestions: Kay Carolyn Brooks, University of Southern Mississippi; Barbara H. Cohen, California State University, Long Beach; Patricia Kolar, University of Pittsburgh; and Sylvia Navari, California State University, Sacramento.

Most of all, I owe a deep debt of gratitude to the many clients who have opened their lives to me and my students. They taught me about real life and how to live it.

IN THE FIELD

CHAPTER 1

BEFORE YOU EMBARK
ON YOUR JOURNEY

When you begin field work, you will learn how to conduct interviews and do assessments. Later you will learn to work in an array of settings and with many different populations. What you learn in your internship is important because it provides the foundation for future learning. You bring to your field placement four things: (1) your appetite for learning, (2) the "book knowledge" you received in classes, (3) your general comfort with people, (4) your learned and innate people skills, and (5) your common sense and natural wisdom.

Remember, everything you do in the field placement and in the associated classroom sessions, even your thoughts as you go to and from the placement, are all rich with learning opportunities. Even the most negative situations can, and will, be beneficial to you as learning experiences. Current junior and senior social work students and former social work students were asked to rank a list of issues and concerns they faced in the field. Later we had the opportunity to do the same with graduate school social work students. This list of twenty-one skills is the result of that task and is offered to provide a framework for some of the challenges facing social work students in the field.

TWENTY-ONE SKILLS YOU WILL LEARN

1. Trusting yourself and your instincts
2. Learning how to learn from your environment
3. Preparing for new and unknown situations
4. Setting the stage for positive relationships
5. Dealing with fears and anxiety
6. Understanding and dealing with agency politics
7. Dealing with loss of idealistic ideas
8. "Finding your voice" with clients
9. Meeting paperwork requirements
10. Handling difficult clients and coworkers
11. Getting the most from your mentors

12. Channeling your anger in positive ways
13. Staying calm in the face of others' anger
14. Turning negative situations into positives
15. Understanding transference and countertransference
16. Strengthening your boundaries
17. Making your age and experience (or lack thereof) work for you
18. Exiting gracefully
19. Evaluating what you've learned
20. Learning to think critically about your work with clients
21. Understanding that learning does not end with field work

TERMINOLOGY USED IN THIS BOOK: CLIENTS, PATIENTS, CONSUMERS

For years, professionals in the human services have debated what to call the individuals they help. In hospitals, the word *patient* is generally used, and in some mental health settings, that word is often preferred. The terminology changes from setting to setting, and varies according to geographic location as well.

In recent years, some have insisted that the word *patient* was demeaning and disempowering. Using the word *client* instead was an attempt to help individuals feel less like victims of the system, and to remind helping professionals that a patient designation does not suggest that individuals deserve inadequate treatment or poor quality service because of a label they are given.

Currently, more and more human services professionals use the term *client;* sometimes the word *consumer* is used to help individuals recognize that they are consumers of services and that they have rights, just as they do in using or purchasing any other service.

In social work practice, the term *client* is generally used rather than *patient* or *consumer.* The Code of Ethics of the National Association of Social Workers states: "Social workers promote social justice and social change with and on behalf of clients. 'Clients' is used inclusively to refer to individuals, families, groups, organizations, and communities." Accordingly, when writing about the individuals you will be helping in social work field placements, I have used the word *client* in this book.

As a student, please keep in mind two ideas about terminology: (1) Regardless of your personal feelings, while you are in your field placement, be flexible and use the term preferred by your supervisor, your setting, and the individuals you work with. (2) Whatever terminology you use, give your clients the best quality service you are capable of, help them to obtain their rights, and treat them with the utmost care, dignity, and respect.

HOW TO GET THE MOST FROM THIS BOOK

This book is not designed to be a bible to be followed chapter by chapter; rather, it is to be used where the student needs to begin. In social work, we use the phrase "Begin where the client is"; you can use this book to begin wherever you need to begin. Each person comes to the task with different levels of skill, knowledge, confidence, and comfort, so feel free to use this book in any way that is helpful to you.

You might want to skim the table of contents and the index to find topics you need to read immediately. You'll probably skip around as you read.

Feel free to write notes to yourself in the margins, dog-ear the pages, use paper clips, high-lighters, or rubber bands to mark important pages or passages. If a particular idea or technique doesn't work for you, don't assume you misunderstood it or failed to apply it properly. Remember that different ideas work for different social workers, and that each client is different from every other client. What works with one client may not work with another. What is important is to begin building and learning new skills and techniques to experiment with.

The word *experiment* suggests that you will not be able to do things perfectly the first time you try. You will flounder, make mistakes, and often feel foolish. You will get the most from your field placement if you are courageous enough to step forward into new territory instead of staying totally safe with material you already know.

THE "RIDE OF YOUR LIFE"

Learning processes can be bitter-sweet experiences, and interns often grow stronger from difficult and uncomfortable situations. This book will not take away your difficulties, but it will help you to be prepared with some basic knowledge and insights into the human condition. You will have a better chance to learn than you might have because you have invested your time and energy in preparing for "the ride of your life"—learning to be a social worker.

Becoming a social worker is a learning adventure that has no beginning or end: Consciously or unconsciously, you've been preparing for this internship all your life, and you will continue to learn and grow throughout your career as a social worker. Remember: You already know much more than you think you know. As you get oriented in your new placement and begin to relax, your *inner* wisdom and all the messages your parents, teachers, and mentors have taught you will begin to come to the surface. You'll get more and more comfortable with yourself, and you'll learn to (1) apply the new skills and techniques, (2) let your *inner* wisdom manifest itself, and (3) blend together your common sense and skills.

Fact of life: We all learn differently, and at different rates of speed. Stop comparing your progress to the student next to you at the placement, or to your friends in other settings. You have different life experiences than they do, and the process will be different for you than for them.

Caution: Be wary of making comparisons. Look only at your own progress, or you'll get distracted from what you're here to do, and from the material you're learning, and from the agency you're fitting into. Yes, it is true, you may have spent your entire life comparing yourself to your siblings, your neighbors, the classmates next to you in Spanish. If you'll remember, comparisons did not help then, and they will help even less now. Comparing will only make you more nervous and anxious and get in the way of learning and being able to see the full picture. If you find yourself in this dark place of comparisons, talk to people you trust for validation. Speak to your supervisor and your college professor responsible for you and your agency placement. Discuss these feelings and explore simple solutions with them to get yourself in to a better emotional state.

DOING YOUR HOMEWORK

You will feel more comfortable if you have researched your new placement before you begin. If you were going on a job interview at a local company, it would be helpful to know the products it produces, how they market, and their source of funding. Being prepared will lower your discomfort to some extent. You will sweat less in the first few days, and, more importantly, it will be easier to ask questions and learn when you are not paralyzed by your own anxiety. The better you understand the product and processes of the agency, the better you will feel going to your new placement. Some of the areas to research include: In what kind of physical building or buildings is the agency located? Who owns the building, or who pays the rent? What is the funding source? How do individuals get access to the services? Are there criteria that determine eligibility for services? This information will give you a general impression of the agency and the clients they serve.

You can get detailed information about the agency from your school or directly from the agency itself. Often, you will find community directories containing helpful information about local agencies. These and other sources can be found in community libraries. Ask your college librarians for assistance, and they will direct you to the materials or tell you how to access the information on the Internet. Of course, the more people and students you can talk to who are familiar with the agency, the more insight you may gain about how you will fit in your new placement.

Depending on your college and the agency, you may have the opportunity to see the placement and have an interview. This is not always possible, in which case you will need to cover these questions when you arrive at the agency. The order of the questions is less important than your feeling comfortable asking for this basic information.

PLACEMENT INTERVIEW QUESTIONS

Do I have a work space?

Is there a break room?

Where can I put my bag, books, and snack or lunch?

Is there any material I can read about the clientele?

What time do you want me here to start the day?

Can I get a list of the staff and their titles?

If I have to call in and you (the supervisor) are not here, whom should I ask to speak to?

If you (the supervisor) are not here and a pressing issue or problem comes up that I can't handle, what should I do?

Do I need any special materials?

What is the dress code and are the clothes I am wearing appropriate?

Do I need to sign in and out?

Are breaks and lunch at a set time?

Where is the bathroom and do I need a key?

If I am out for any reason, can I make up the time?

Where do I park my car? Is there a parking fee? Do I need a parking pass?

I will be using public transportation; can you tell me the nearest train/bus stop?

What are the expected hours of my placement?

Can I adjust my schedule to match the train/bus schedule?

If I think of any other questions can I call you? #_____

PREPARING YOUR ATTITUDES

One of the most important things you can do to prepare for field work is to review your basic philosophies and attitudes. Showing up with a cooperative and helpful attitude will go a long way toward dealing with any fears or anxieties you may have.

> Everything is a learning opportunity. Say "yes" to what life has to teach you.

Work at remaining nonjudgmental, even in your own thoughts. Stay in a mentally neutral, "observer" position. If you are constantly running "software" through your mind that says, "This guy's a jerk" or "That woman is crazy," your attitude will almost certainly "leak out" on some level and be perceived by the people around you. Remember that you are new to the field, and when you are more experienced and have more information about particulars, you may understand better why a supervisor, a coworker, or a client has acted in a particular way. Remind yourself, also, that supervisors and others often have personal stresses and pressures that may cause them to behave in less-than-perfect ways. They may have health concerns, family problems, problems with employees, or hassles and frustrations within the system, so give them the benefit of the doubt, just as you would like to be treated yourself. It costs you nothing to "put the best face" on a situation and refrain from judging. An old saying to keep in mind is: "Seek truth, pardon error." Think also that, given the same circumstances, you might act in exactly the same way. This attitude will serve as the foundation for your actions and behaviors.

> "The art of wisdom is in knowing what to ignore."

Be teachable. Be humble. Know your limitations and be able to talk about them. It is usually better to enter a field placement (as well as a new job) with an attitude that suggests that you don't know everything there is to know and that you are willing to learn. In general, supervisors are not nearly as concerned with what you know or don't know as with your ability to cooperate and work as part of a team. Most supervisors would rather have a willing student who is not well trained than a super-competent one who will not listen, learn, or cooperate. Better to say "I don't know what to do in this situation, can you help me?" than to pretend to be more competent than you feel or to barge in without knowing what you're doing or asking for help.

> Learn to be a Social Worker first.

Remember that you will make mistakes, and that they are an important part of the learning process. Don't try to cover them up. Ask for help, and learn how "do it right" the next time.

Don't take things personally. It may not be about you. Often, when someone is angry with you or behaves badly because of something you said or did, that person is angry with someone else and you just happen to be there. Your actions cannot cause others to feel a particular way or do a certain thing—that's their responsibility. Remember: "They're not doing it to you, they're just doing it."

Listen deeply, be fully present, and work at understanding what is said to you before you disagree or object. Be cooperative. When you disagree with your supervisor or a coworker, it is often wise to postpone your negative reactions. Instead, "buy time," by saying something like, "What you've said sounds very important, so I'd like to think about it first before I act on it." This lets your supervisor know that you are carefully considering the message, and that your disagreement isn't an impulsive, thoughtless gesture. In the meantime, you may gain a deeper understanding of the issue, and be able to formulate your response in a nonangry, nonthreatening, cooperative way. You may also be able to work out a compromise based on discussion and deeper understanding from you both.

Stay out of controversies that don't concern you. As a student, you're in a unique situation to observe without the level of involvement of a staff member. Although agency politics may be uncomfortable, it's important to learn to let problems have their proper place without affecting you. Remember the old saying, "Like water off a duck's back." Let other people's unpleasantness roll off you while you take care of your own business.

An important lesson to learn is how to use every opportunity as a learning tool. You can learn just as much or more from a negative encounter with someone as from a pleasant one. Remember the incident, and learn from it. It is likely that some day in the future, you will become a supervisor and these events now are part of your training and preparation for a higher level of authority in the future.

Through your words, actions, tone of voice, attitudes, and body posture, convey to your supervisor and coworkers that:

> You're here to learn, not complain.
> You're here to listen, not talk.
> You're a team player, not a prima donna.
> You're here to meet the clients' needs, not your own.
> You'll respect the supervisor, even if you disagree.
> You're willing to do what it takes to get the job done.
> You're dependable.

Use a diary or a journal to assess your own strengths and weaknesses as you would assess your client. Then look at the techniques or defenses you use in conjunction with your weaknesses. Do these techniques and tools enhance your learning, or are they geared to protect you and help you avoid confronting uncomfortable knowledge about yourself? If your supervisor is less than complimentary during a supervisory meeting, how might you respond? You might want to practice responding in your journal before you talk to your supervisor. By that time, you will probably have calmed down and become more objective. Ask yourself whether there is at least some truth in the information you are being given. The key here is to create an ability to hear what is being stated, then work with (not against) that information in order to grow as a social worker.

BUILDING YOUR PROFESSIONAL WARDROBE

In planning what to wear, it would be helpful to know if there is an agency dress code. Often, within the dress code, there is a level of formality that your agency is comfortable with. What kind of clothing does your supervisor wear? How are your coworkers dressed? It is important to "blend in," rather than call attention to clothing that is extreme. If you have little knowledge of the particular placement, ask your teacher or fellow students who have been in field work.

In general, think about what you would wear for a job interview and plan your professional wardrobe accordingly. Do not feel that you need to rush out and spend a lot of money to buy a whole new set of clothes. The contents of your closet can probably be updated with little or no money. Take inventory of the suitable clothing you already own and make a list of anything you need to add.

> Strapped for cash? It's a little-known secret that if you know how to shop carefully, you can build an appropriate professional wardrobe by shopping at thrift stores, where you can get everything you need for an amazingly low price. If you're not sure how to do this, ask a fashion-conscious friend to go shopping with you. Your friend will appreciate the challenge and can advise you about what looks good on you.

One important issue with regard to clothing has to do with complying with safety regulations at your agency. By now, you should be familiar with the guidelines, or if you're not, ask your supervisor for a copy. Some agencies discourage or forbid high heels, dangling earrings, neckties, necklaces, or scarves.

In any case, dress in good taste, and in a way that is comfortable for you. In the first few days of your placement, it may be better to err on the side of formality than informality. You can always relax your standards once you are settled, but it would be embarrassing to be taken aside and told your torn cutoffs are a no-no.

A male student and I did not have the opportunity to meet before the placement began, which may have contributed to the problem. When we met the first day of the placement, the student was dressed in a wrinkled cotton shirt and blue jeans. The professional staff at this setting were all dressed in causal, yet dressy clothes—sport coats and ties for the men and dresses or dress slacks, tops, and jackets for the females. Not only did the student not dress professionally for this placement, it was clear that, even after a few days, he had not noticed that his clothing did not fit in with the staff. I called him into the office to discuss his clothing. After a short conversation, it was clear this student did own the appropriate attire but lacked awareness of the dress issue. This was not a good way to begin his placement with a new supervisor.

In particular, female students need to dress modestly. That means no plunging necklines, short or slit skirts, exposed midriffs, or tight clothing. You may be working with clients with poor impulse control or who may think your fashionable clothes are "sexy." They may even think you are sending sexual signals to them when you are just dressing in fashion.

On the first day of placement, a female student wore a tight, cleavage-revealing blouse. A male client came over to her and stared at her chest while engaged in conversation with her. Shortly after the incident, she came to my office in tears. Yes, the male client should not have done what he did; however, she, as a student, did not dress appropriately or professionally.

There are times and situations when you can dress down but still maintain good professional boundaries. This is essential whether you are working with clients at the agency, at a picnic, or on a therapeutic outing.

Ask for guidance about dress for special occasions. For example, there is a summer program during which emotionally handicapped adolescents go to a local pool several times a week. The staff there are not permitted to wear bathing suits or use the pool. Clearly, this program is concerned about professional boundaries and uses its dress code to reinforce them.

In addition to dress, check your mannerisms and use of humor. Students who act with their clients as they might with friends often confuse their clients. They may mistake your humor and friendliness for flirtation. In your dress and manner, convey maturity, seriousness, and professionalism. Be careful not to send mixed signals. Clients may confuse your friendliness with sexual availability.

THE MATURE STUDENT

When we were preparing to write this guide to field work, I met with former students to discuss the content of the book. Several of the students were older than the average bachelor-degree student and they felt there should be a section devoted to the more mature student. I recall joking that this section should be in bigger print, for those needing reading glasses. All social work students share common concerns and issues, but there are variations in how those issues are played out in field work placements that are impacted by age and experience issues.

As you travel through life you gather your personal history. It is as if you store it in a backpack you carry. Younger students often have less life experience in their backpacks than older ones. In addition to life history, including learning experiences, good and bad, the "backpack" includes responsibilities you have collected, which may include a spouse, children, aging parents, debts, and one or more jobs.

Older students can appear more poised, more confident, and generally better equipped than their younger counterparts. Often this life experience can be misleading, creating a belief that the mature student is more prepared. In spite of this appearance, remember that both older and younger students have taken the same classes and have the same level of experience in social work. However, being more experienced in life situations, older students will often not show their inner anxiety and uncertainty on the outside. The fact that you can hide your nervousness does not necessarily mean you are better prepared than other students. Furthermore, your calm may be a disadvantage in that it may mislead your supervisor into thinking you are more skilled than you really are.

> I was supervising an older student. She struggled through the first semester, eventually reaching the evaluation process. As she and I went over each area of her evaluation, she became increasingly agitated. When I addressed this behavior, she explained that she did not agree with my ratings and felt she should have gotten better ones. The student was unable to hear the message of her evaluation clearly. I reviewed the process and explained that she was expected neither to be an expert at this point in her training, nor to have learned all the tasks well at mid-year. She left the room very upset and eager to seek out her fellow students for emotional support.

All students need to learn to be their own advocates, but confronting a supervisor without understanding the whole picture can be self-destructive. So, where is the line she crossed? With each rating, examples were given that came from her process recording and supervisory conversations in which she discussed her work with her clients.

Was the supervisor unfair? Had she been misled prior to her evaluation? I will leave these questions unanswered for now. In this student's case, she responded aggressively and repeatedly argued her viewpoint.

Mature students bring baggage that can both help and hinder them in their placements. The key is to know when your life experiences enrich and when they are a liability. You must also know how and when to apply your skills. Many supervisors would rather have teachable, humble students of any age than opinionated ones who believe they already know what they need to know. It is often easier to teach an unskilled person than to work with someone who must be "untaught" ideas or practices that do not fit the setting.

You may feel more comfortable with the agency staff if you are close to their ages, and they may even speak to you in a different manner than they would to someone much younger. It is an easy trap for staff persons to treat you as a peer and forget you are inexperienced in social work. Don't misinterpret this familiarity to mean you are a peer: Be clear in your role as a student. Make it clear that, despite your age, you are still there to learn.

If you are older than your supervisor, you might want to make it very clear that you acknowledge the supervisor's position and experience. Emphasize that you are able and willing to learn from someone younger than you. Your supervisor may be relieved that you won't automatically be a source of difficulty just because of the age difference.

Life experience can give a second-career student more people skills to be used with clients, supervisors, and agency staff. An older student may be better equipped, less anxious, and less intimidated by new situations such as an agency setting.

Experience can also be a mixed blessing in sessions with your clients. Your know-how may help you understand situations your clients bring to sessions; however, to assume you understand because you have also had experience in the same area is a trap. For example, your client tells you how it feels to have to force a child to do homework. As a parent, you can relate, but don't assume you have experienced what the client has experienced.

HOUSE RULES

Each placement comes with its own set of requirements. These requirements may seem silly or boring but they are there to protect you, the staff, and the clients who receive services at that agency. There may be an orientation requirement that involves listening to speakers and videotapes on an array of topics from employee safety to infection control issues. If there is an orientation process listen carefully: Are there any codes for medical emergency or a code for "need help," client at risk of hurting someone? What is the fire safety policy of your placement? What are you to do in an emergency? Call 911 or the safety department? Is there a list of emergency numbers, fire, police, and ambulance? I am speaking in broad terms because the range of placements is so great. Importantly, if the agency does not have a formal orientation process, sit down with your supervisor and review these issues.

Some agencies require staff to sign in. This is a way to account for who is in the building and could prove vital in an emergency such as a fire or hazardous spill. Sound ridiculous? Well several of my students were in a building that had an unidentified chemical spill. The building was evacuated and everyone needed to be accounted for. They may require you to wear an ID badge to help the clients identify the staff.

Some agencies are very formal in the manner clients and staff are addressed, others are less formal. You will need to be alert to the policy of your placement, whether stated formally or informally. This can be an important boundary issue with certain client populations. Ask your supervisor what is appropriate.

Check to find out the policy on the use of cell phones and pages. Some agencies forbid their use; others have no policy. But before your cell phone goes off while at your placement, know the policy. Even in the absence of an agency policy, there may be times when it is inappropriate for your cell phone to ring or your pager to beep, e.g., while with a client, in supervision, or a staff meeting.

What I have not mentioned here are the policies for record keeping and confidentiality. These topics are covered more extensively under the topics of paperwork and confidentiality, including the Health Insurance Portability and Accountability Act (HIPAA).

SUPERVISION, PLACEMENTS, AND SUPPORT FROM THE COLLEGE

There are certain realities that a student must often face. Over the years, we have all heard stories about difficulties with field work as well as the wonderful moments. Situations range from the student being assigned no clients or groups, or limited supervisor time, to students reporting quality supervision and support from other staff. There may be supervisors you wish you'd never known and others with whom you'll want to keep in touch with after your placement. So the amount of support you get during field work can vary a great deal. One problem is that students often struggle, but for one reason or another, do not talk to their supervisors or professors about their needs.

> We expect our clients to make their needs known: Doesn't that same rule apply to social work students?

Ideally, your field work will be connected to your college classroom assignments. There are times when students start a placement not in sequence with class time. If you are one of these students, you can feel very isolated. Make an effort to stay in touch with the college field work advisor, via e-mail or face-to-face. The how is less important than the connection. You must advocate for yourself and inform your supervisor of your needs over the course of the year. Neither supervisors nor professors are mind readers. I began teaching in the fall semester with several students who were in two different placements. Two students were in a counseling center for the summer and were assigned groups that were actively running weekly. These students were being supervised and had plenty of material for class discussion and process recordings. Several other students were placed in a shelter program for the summer. There was less structure and the on-site supervisor had been transferred. The students were not engaged in any client work and they had not brought this to the college field work faculty. Additionally, these students were short of the required number of field work hours. This example illustrates that there are times you need to advocate for yourself.

> I recall a student who was in supervision with a colleague in my agency. After their supervision sessions, the student was in tears. The supervisor, concerned with the progress the student was making, came to me asking for peer supervision. Let me quickly point out that whether the supervision was good or a bad is irrelevant at this point. What he was doing was using an important social work skill: seeking peer supervision. In this particular case, one of the interventions was for the supervisor to contact the college and discuss the issues with the field work supervisor. The student was also encouraged to speak to his field work advisor.

Field work placements are difficult enough without having a strained relationship with your supervisor. Later, I will discuss in detail a concept called Mirror-Mirror; however, it needs to be mentioned briefly now. Your relationship with your supervisor mirrors your relationship with your clients (also known as parallel process). If you are in a less-than-trusting relationship with your supervisor, feeling vulnerable, how can you be honest and share your experiences openly? The same is true for your clients. They need to trust you so they can feel safe enough to be honest with you about their needs.

Every placement has the potential for both positive and not-so-positive situations. Even a difficult placement, however, can be rich in learning experience. If you find yourself in a negative placement, you must talk to your college faculty advisors as well as your peers. They need to know what you are going through, and they can give you helpful strategies to survive. Again, you must learn to advocate for yourself. You need to seek effective support, because you can't learn if you are an emotional wreck.

With that in mind, what should you do if you are concerned that you can't handle the placement and you are frightened or hate your supervisor? You must advocate for yourself and let your supervisor or the college field advisor know what you are experiencing. The worst thing you can do is nothing. If you are anxious or frightened, speak to your supervisor. They are there to guide you. Remember, they are not mind readers. Sometimes frequent short contacts or interventions with your supervisor can help you. Some supervisors are open to students stopping by to share their daily experience. Others are more formal and prefer scheduled times to meet. In either case, be prepared with your questions and your concerns. The more open you can be about your personal experience as a social work intern, the better your supervisor can mentor and guide you.

There are different ways to get supervision. You already know the formal supervisory model: You have a set time to meet with your supervisor and discuss process recordings and other issues. There are other paths to supervision that you will experience as well. There are eager professionals in the agency who often lend a hand, perhaps the co-leader of your support group. You may be overwhelmed by the new agency record system, only to find there are staff who are very good teachers of these tasks. Often you do not have to seek them out; if you show interest they will often offer their services.

LEARNING CONTRACTS

Learning contracts are a part of the supervisory experience and many colleges require students to outline their learning goals while with that agency. Some students see this as a daunting task; others find it very easy. This is a skill that you will need to learn in any case. This is reflective of the work you will be doing with your clients. What are their goals and how will you know they are achieved?

Sit down with your supervisor. Discuss the agency goals and goals for their clients. You now have at least one learning goal: to understand the complex goals of your clients. Explore the goal by developing a plan as to how you will achieve the goal. Will you have a caseload of clients? How many clients? Will you be assigned to run groups? Are you to do home visits? Let us not forget that every agency has its professional jargon that you will need to learn. Finally, you are there to learn how to conform to the professional standards and ethical behavior of the social work profession. All of these questions and issues, their answers and practical solutions, will come to comprise the components of the learning contract.

The value of a learning contract is that it tells you what you are to learn and how you will achieve these goals. It sets the course and guides you. It can help you determine when you are on track and when redirection is necessary. It helps you and your supervisor focus on your internship. Embedded within this contract are the tools to achieve the goals, such as your supervisor advocating for you, the student, to be assigned a client that will be an excellent learning opportunity, or advocating that you be allowed to sit in on a case conference, or to go with the team of professionals on a home visit. The learning contract can also help you to identify when you need to advocate for yourself with your supervisor to achieve the goals.

NOTES TO YOURSELF

Reminders of things to do: _____

_____

_____

_____

_____

_____

_____

Situations that relate to readings: _____

_____

_____

_____

_____

_____

_____

Questions to ask your supervisor: _____

_____

_____

_____

_____

_____

_____

Supervisor's comments: _____

_____

_____

_____

_____

_____

_____

■ ■ ■ ■ ■

CHAPTER 2

MAKING THE LEAP FROM THEORY TO REAL LIFE

EMOTIONAL READINESS: "STANDING IN THE RAIN"

You can study the physical and chemical properties of rain. You can measure its impact on the environment. You can possess an intimate book-knowledge of rain down to its molecules. But what does it feel like to stand in the rain and feel the drops on your face?

In a like manner, you learn social work theories and techniques in the classroom; you read and discuss; you role-play; you study the research literature; and you test your knowledge. You have an intimate book-knowledge of social work, but what does it feel like to be a social worker?

Most students will make every effort to look and sound ready for their placement. They will often buy new clothing and evaluate their current wardrobe to make sure it looks professional. But you and I know your quaking inner world may not match your confident exterior. Most students will tell you they feel very unprepared for their first day, and they may even say they feel vulnerable, helpless, and even "stupid" in their new settings.

These feelings are all natural and normal. When you begin a whole new level of learning (which field work certainly is), you tend to regress to earlier emotional states. It is not unusual to panic and feel like you're three years old, even with a supportive supervisor and many people surrounding you, reminding you, "You can do it. You have what it takes."

When I began to write this book, I interviewed many students about their beginning field work experiences. I also talked to new and experienced social workers in various stages of their careers. I found similar feelings among undergraduate juniors preparing to enter their first field placement and seniors beginning their second placement. What may surprise you is that I heard the same feelings expressed by graduate students, social workers beginning their first jobs, and even seasoned workers who have changed settings or experienced changes in the structure of their work.

> Remember: There will be new emotional pressures any time you learn, grow, or expose yourself to a new environment, no matter how much support you have. So don't underestimate the impact your new placement will have on you.

For example, one student talked about how intensely he prepared for his first internship by talking to the student who had just completed his field work at the same setting. They discussed in detail the agency staff, the clients served, and even the particular clients that would be assigned to the new student. Even with all this prior knowledge, the new student's experience was quite different from the person who had just left.

Another social work student did all the prior homework she could, investigating the agency and their funding sources, and speaking to two former students of that agency about the clients and the work. Halfway through the year, she noted how unprepared she felt for what she actually experienced in the field.

You wonder, if these students did their homework as this book suggests and your college professors tell you to do, how is it possible they still felt so unprepared? The answer is simple: The preparatory activities the students did were intellectual, and their experiences in the field were loaded with emotional content.

"Standing in the rain" or beginning a field work placement is a totally new experience. Its first effect on you will be to make you feel inadequate and ill-prepared. That's not at all true, but the flooding of emotions leads you to believe you're not up to the new challenges. Just take a deep breath, and remind yourself that you are not any of the things above. You are simply in another universe called field work agency placement. Welcome to all the new experiences and feelings.

A student came to class reporting how much she enjoyed her placement and how great it was that she could do intake assessments on all the new clients. She was feeling very comfortable with the placement, not realizing she was doing a task she was very familiar with from her previous job. Regardless of why her supervisor allowed this situation to happen, it is more important you understand the problem from the student's perspective. We all gravitate toward activities that are comfortable to us, so in this case the student was doing nothing wrong. However, the student was not being given tasks that were new and unfamiliar to her. This kind of situation is a disservice to the student, who needs to experience new learning situations that will probably be more uncomfortable than familiar ones.

If you're a mature student returning to school or beginning a second or even third career, you may feel that it will be easier for you to "stand in the rain." Actually, this metaphor may apply to you even more than to the average student because you're taking "backward steps" in putting yourself in a "one-down" position after you've been accustomed to a higher rung on the career ladder.

One final note about emotional readiness. You will never be fully pre-pared for what is to come. You will never have all the confidence or infor-mation you want and need. That's life. What's important to remember is that your feelings are natural and normal and that you can still move forward and learn what you need to learn despite your fears and negative emotions.

UNDERSTANDING THE PROCESS OF CHANGE

It is important to understand how people change for two reasons. First, you need to know how to help your clients make constructive changes in their lives, and second, you need to understand your own processes of learning and growing as you progress through your field work placement. You're going through a parallel process with your clients: You're changing your life by training to become a social worker, and they're attempting to make vari-ous positive changes in their own lives.

There is a common misconception about how people make improve-ments in their lives. The bootstrap philosophy of "Just Do It," suggests that:

- Changing is simple and easy.
- All it takes is will power.
- It's an either/or process: Either you're changing or you're not.
- If you've tried and failed, something must be wrong with you.

James Prochaska, John Norcross, and Carlo DiClemente consolidated their findings on the process of change in their book: *Changing for Good: A Revolution-ary Six-Stage Program for Overcoming Bad Habits and Moving Your Life Positively For-ward* (1995). According to the authors, change involves six stages, but nothing actually happens until stage four: Action. Up to that point, there is no outward evidence that change is taking place. However, if the essential groundwork has not been laid in the preceding Precontemplation, Contemplation, and Prepara-tion phases, any actions you take in the fourth stage of Action are likely to fail.

The Six Stages of Change:

1. Precontemplation—Not thinking about change at all—denial—getting fed up with yourself
2. Contemplation—Thinking about changing—considering it
3. Preparation—Getting ready to change—laying the mental groundwork for change
4. Action—Actually making the needed changes
5. Maintenance—Maintaining the changes you're making
6. Termination—The problem behaviors are no longer an issue—no need to think about them

From: *Changing for Good* by Prochaska, Norcross, & DiClemente (1995).

There are many models of the change process, but two key elements in this model suggest why so many people fail at making important changes in their lives: (1) they haven't understood the underlying structure of the change process, and (2) they haven't gotten enough of the right kind of support for each stage of growth.

Don't be upset with yourself when you occasionally slip backward. That's to be expected from time to time. Remember that, just as your clients need your emotional support, you also need to make sure you are setting up support systems for yourself such as teachers, your supervisor, advisors, peers, support groups as needed, and trusted colleagues.

MISTAKES: ERRORS OF TECHNIQUE
VERSUS ERRORS OF THE HEART

Before their first field placement, many students worry whether they possess enough knowledge. They often are certain that they do not know nearly enough about theories and techniques. Remember this old saying: "Our clients will forgive us for errors of technique, but they will never forgive us for errors of the heart." If your heart is "in the right place;" if you sincerely want to help your clients, and if you are humble enough to admit your mistakes and apologize, you will learn the techniques you need as you go along.

> A client wanted me to help him make a phone call. Being very new in my placement, I was afraid that would be against the rules or somehow inappropriate. I told him "no," because we had to concentrate on my agenda. He became angry with me, and seemed to withdraw and "shut down." I didn't have a good feeling about the situation. When I talked to my supervisor, she suggested I apologize to him and help him make the call as soon as possible. He seemed relieved when I told him how sorry I was that I did the wrong thing. We made the call, and ever after he was much more open and cooperative. My apology seemed to make a huge difference in the quality of our therapeutic relationship. Even though it was hard to admit I was in the wrong, my supervisor helped me to correct a serious error.

What you have learned from your classes and textbooks is very important. That knowledge serves as the "base of the pyramid" on which you will build your career. In the helping professions, it is impossible to learn everything you need to know from books and classes; you learn by doing. You learn by experience, by "getting your feet wet," by observing, and by making mistakes. Life and your clients will continue to teach you what you need to know throughout your career. You will keep on learning and growing, no matter how many years of experience you attain. Just keep your mind and heart open, and the lessons will appear.

Treating your clients with respect and dignity is essential to being a good social worker. Your clients know when you are sincere and truly want what is best for them, without the exact words ever spoken.

Shortly, we will begin to share some actual process recordings with you to illustrate certain points with "real life" experiences. Note that these recordings are not necessarily the "ideal" way to handle a situation, but an example of how an intern actually reacted.

FOUR KINDS OF PAPERWORK

You will find at least four categories of paperwork activities occurring at the same time. First are the papers you need to produce for your college or university. Make your on-site supervisor aware of these in order to give them time to direct you if you need assistance. This may begin in the form of a learning contract, which many colleges require. Come to your supervisor for input with plenty of time to spare. If you ask for help when your paperwork is due in just a few days, you get little or no help. You will also be sending the message that you are not responsible enough to plan ahead, keep track of your tasks, and complete them in an orderly fashion. Your supervisor may be very helpful if given time to think about what you need.

The second kind of paperwork is advocacy for your clients, including Social Security forms, lost green cards, unemployment papers, department of social services forms, public assistance, or any other kinds of paperwork they need help with. Some of this kind of paperwork strikes at the heart of what it means to be a social worker. Often referred to as concrete services, this kind of paperwork is crucial to your clients' well-being. This is one of the things social workers do: We advocate for our clients. We help them do things they need help with. Ask your supervisor or other staff about the common types of advocacy paperwork at your agency.

The third type of paperwork is the documentation paperwork required by your agency. Documentation is a critical part of agency work and it is important to remember that each piece of paperwork becomes a legal document. It is important that you understand the documentation needs of your agency from day one. The kind of paperwork you will do will depend on what kind of agency you have been placed with. For example federal, state, private, not-for-profit, school-based, specialty programs, or grants, just to name a few, all have different requirements.

Becoming increasingly popular is the electronic record keeping system. While visiting someone in the hospital you may have seen the nurse take a patient's vitals and then enter that information on a key board and monitor in the patient's room. Some electronic record keeping systems are partial, meaning the complete client record is not computerized. An example of this partial record could be tracking vitals. In other systems, the entire client record is computerized.

Access to the computerized client records is well guarded to protect clients from any breach in confidential information, so your access may be limited. On the other hand, if you are expected to complete these computerized forms, you will go through the process of being granted access. This can involve signing forms stating that you will protect against others gaining access, fingerprinting for scanners, and passwords that often need to be changed. Often this process is conducted in training sessions.

> Your client's chart is a legal document and needs to be treated with care. This means: be neat, make sure your content is accurate, and that it presents your client in his or her best light.

Many supervisors encourage their students to read client records to get an idea of the kinds of paperwork needed. If your supervisor does not offer to show you actual client records, you might ask to see examples of the completed paperwork you will be required to do so you will know exactly what is expected of you. Ask questions. For example, do the forms or paperwork have detailed categories to fill in the blanks or are they free-form? Make notes on a blank form or make yourself an outline to follow. Show the outline to your supervisor for completeness. Rewrites are time-consuming and not a rewarding activity, even though you will often find yourself doing them. You will need to know what forms to use, and how often they are to be completed.

WRITING CHART NOTES

Generally speaking, each time you have contact with a client, whether in a structured, face-to-face session, a telephone conversation, or even a significant interaction in the hallway, that contact will need to be documented. Some of this may be related to Medicare and Medicaid billing and cross-checking a fact of life. The important point to remember is that your documentation in the chart is leaving a trail of activity. This is valuable if someone needs to work with your client in your absence. They will have a record of your contacts and what you have been discussing. You will find value weeks or months later when you and your client reflect on progress. You will have the documentation to trace the progress or lack thereof.

If not offered, ask to see client records to begin to understand the forms the agency uses, the intervals forms that need to be completed, and the structure of notes. In some placements, students are asked to write their notes in rough draft form on scrap paper. Their notes are then reviewed by the supervisor, with input to help them rewrite the note. In some cases, a supervisor might rewrite the note or help them put it into final form. When you have demonstrated your ability to write acceptable notes, you may have less supervision concerning them.

Other supervisors may discuss the needed content of a note and then let you write it on your own. Remember: You haven't written chart notes before. This will be your first time, so don't expect to write a perfect note. Soon you'll become comfortable with the process and be able to write notes that fulfill your agency's requirements.

PROGRESS NOTES

The purpose of a progress note is to document the client's progress or lack of progress toward particular goals. Ask your supervisor about what you say and don't say in a progress note. As these are legal documents, you must always keep in mind that it is possible that some day, your note or notes may be read out loud in a court room, so write the note accordingly. Ask your supervisor how brief or expanded the notes should be. Given current changes in privacy laws, some agencies prefer that you document as briefly as possible in order to protect the rights of the client.

Another possibility is that, at some point, clients may ask to read their own charts. In the past, it was rare that clients would be given permission to read their records, but state and federal laws are changing on this issue. Would you be comfortable with your client reading what you have written about him or her?

Regardless of the format of the note, make sure that, above all, the content of the note is accurate. Take care to document only what is necessary, and consult with your supervisor if you think the content of a note might harm the client now or in the future. For the future protection of the client, you may be asked to write notes in a vague, summarized fashion. For example, you might not write in detail about fantasies or other dynamic psychological issues or anything that might inadvertently prejudice a less understanding worker against the client.

Whatever you decide to put into your notes, you have a moral, ethical, and potentially legal responsibility to report and record with as much accuracy as possible. This is always true, but especially so when what you report can have a significant impact on the client's future. Reported or suspected criminal activity on the part of the client is an example. A social worker came to me and reported there was an entry in his client's record that reported the client had set fire to his home. The social worker was making a referral for housing for the individual and knew this would affect his getting accepted. This social worker took the time to interview the case manager and others only to find out there had been a fire in the home at an earlier date and it was not set by the client. The reporting of the "arson" in an unchecked form would have impacted this client for the rest of his life. This situation illustrates the importance of validating information the client reports or that you may get from previous records or staff. I don't want to frighten you from note writing, just heighten your understanding that it is not to be taken lightly.

Another important legal issue related to documentation is the use of white-out type products. Do not use any kind of white-out in your forms or notes. The clinical record is a legal document and, as such, cannot be altered in any way. The use of white-out will only render your notes suspect. In other words, people will wonder why the note was changed, for that is what they will think when they see white-out. At worst, you can be accused of falsifying a legal document. There are legal ways to correct legitimate errors made when making chart entries. While your agency may have a specific policy, the general rule to correct errors is to draw a line though the word and write the correct one next to it. Your agency may also require you to initial the correction. Ask your supervisor for the agency's policy or procedure in this area. You may not want to discuss a "mistake" or misspelling with your supervisor, but you will only compound the mistake by using white-out.

Again, don't forget that the client's chart is a legal document, and you do not want to create a situation where someone can say that you were trying to hide something, no matter how trivial the detail or how innocent your motivations.

> A supervisor explains: One of my students was not the best of writers or spellers and had made a spelling mistake in a client's progress note. I read the note she had written and cosigned her signature as is the policy in my agency. A few days later, the client's doctor came to me concerning something written that day by my student that I had not yet reviewed, discussed, and cosigned. When I looked at the new note there was a word that had been whited out, but the situation grew worse when I noticed that the prior note I had cosigned had also been altered with white-out after I cosigned it. Once I stopped hyperventilating, I called the student into my office to explain herself.
>
> The first mistake was that, as a supervisor, I had apparently not made it clear to her that white-out was never to be used. The second error was that the student should never have altered a note that a supervisor had cosigned.
>
> The incident became a learning experience for both the student and for me, as the supervisor. The student was trying to present the best note possible, but ended up with more problems than she had bargained for.

A final comment on client's charts and documents in the client's chart. They are legal documents, and are never to leave the agency without proper authorization. As a student, never remove documents from a client record for your use in a classroom assignment. I have seen a student lose his placement because he took home a client's record to prepare an assignment on cultural differences.

Tips concerning paperwork:

- Know which forms are required on every client and which are not.
- Know how often a form must be completed (every three months, six months, yearly, or every visit).
- Ask for a written reference guide at the agency for structure of notes and forms. Make notes on blank forms if you can, or take careful notes.
- Know what content is needed in a note, and what content should be omitted (and why).
- Know your agency's note format.
- Don't use white-out products.

PROCESS RECORDINGS

The fourth important category of paperwork is your process recordings, a time-honored tradition in social work. Your process recordings are invaluable tools of learning. Your supervisor may give you a form he or she prefers. Generally speaking, there is a basic structure of three columns that can be made up on any computer. Most word-processing software can make tables. Create a simple three-column table that will fill a page in landscape format. If you are stuck, ask a friend to help. The top categories can be arranged as your supervisor prefers. Remember to write your name, the date, and number the pages at the top of the process recording even if you staple the pages together.

HE SAID/SHE SAID	STUDENT FEELINGS	SUPERVISOR COMMENTS

You will fill in the appropriate two columns, and the supervisor will add comments under "Supervisor Comments," either in writing or verbally in the supervision session.

Present yourself to your supervisor as an organized person. When you write your process recording, did you remember to number the pages and put your name and the date on the top of each page? Don't forget to make copies of your process recordings. If your supervisor returns the process recording before you meet, with his or her comments, make a copy of those comments as well. That way, when you meet, you will each have a copy of the same material during the supervision discussion and can easily refer to the same material together.

> My supervisor always tells me, "When you come to supervision bring two copies of the process recording." One of my peers did not do this. He would enter the room with one copy and the supervisor would ask him to go the copier and make another copy. When he returned he would have two copies, but they were now out of order and disorganized. This is not how you want to present yourself to your supervisor.

NOTES TO YOURSELF

Reminders of things to do: _____
_____
_____
_____
_____
_____
_____

Situations that relate to readings: _____
_____
_____
_____
_____
_____
_____

Questions to ask your supervisor: _____
_____
_____
_____
_____
_____
_____

Supervisor's comments: _____
_____
_____
_____
_____
_____
_____

CHAPTER 3

BEGINNING AT THE BEGINNING

THE FIRST DAY

The first few days of field work placement can be harrowing because you may be keyed up and nervous with anticipation, unsure of yourself, self-conscious, and doubting your ability to "measure up." You may not even have had enough sleep because you are so excited and anxious. All these factors make a new situation seem daunting. Some general tips for navigating a new beginning:

Get as much information ahead of time as you can about your placement, the clients, the supervisor, and your coworkers. Talk to others who have been at the same agency before you. The more detailed information you have before the first day, the more prepared you will feel.

Give yourself some time to understand the political environment. Observe quietly, and notice who is aligned with whom, where the real power lies. Be particularly observant in meetings to get a "feel" for what's going on. Be friendly with everyone, but not overly familiar. You may feel lonely and out of place, but don't align quickly with anyone until you get a feel for the political climate. If, for example, you become chummy with someone who doesn't get along with your supervisor, you could be borrowing trouble. Don't allow yourself to get cornered by a coworker with a hidden or not-so-hidden agenda. Listen more than you talk. Be ready for agency staff to ask questions that may put you on the spot.

> It was my first day at the agency. At the end of my first staff meeting, someone asked me what I thought of my placement after the first day. I said I could see that the staff worked well as a team, and I was sure I would get a lot out of my field work here. Half kiddingly and half seriously, the medical director turned to another coworker and laughed. "Well, we fooled another one, didn't we?" I felt a little foolish for answering such a "dangerous" question. It was only weeks later that I began to see how the staff climate was very tense, with workers feeling hostile and angry with one another because of unequal work loads.

Earn your "idiosyncrasy credit" by keeping a low profile for a while. Fit in with the way things are done. Be quiet and cooperative. "Play the game" as you understand it, and make an honest effort to do what seems to be expected of you. After you've been around for a while, your coworkers will trust and respect you more, and you will have earned the right to have your own opinions and personal style. You will be allowed to be "yourself" as a unique individual. For example, some "don'ts:"

- Don't wear loud or unusual clothing.
- Don't talk about yourself.
- Don't discuss your personal problems.
- Don't talk about your boyfriend/girlfriend.
- Keep your weekends to yourself.
- Don't discuss your private life.
- And, above all, don't gossip.

Your differences will be more likely to be tolerated after coworkers have gotten to know and trust you than at the very beginning. Then you'll be seen as "one of us." Be punctual. Better to be a little early than late. Tardiness might be interpreted as laziness, lack of interest, lack of planning, or disorganization. Think ahead and make extra special efforts to be where you're supposed to be on time.

> Don't set things up so you have to be reminded to be somewhere at a certain time by your supervisor. Be "clock conscious" and plan ahead to get there on your own.

Listen and be attentive at meetings. If unfamiliar terms or abbreviations are used, write them down so you can look them up later. Perhaps you can ask your peers or your supervisor at a later time. If you ask elementary questions at a meeting, you may seem unprepared. As you get more and more comfortable over time, you'll feel more like taking risks in asking questions, or making tentative interpretations.

Unless you already know where everyone sits at meetings, wait until most people are seated, or find a place at the back. You may accidentally sit in someone's favorite chair. If you are asked to come forward, that's fine, but it might be embarrassing to be told you're too forward.

> At the first meeting, I was overly eager to show up on time, so I got to the room a little early. I took a chair at the table, and got out my notebook, ready to take notes. Someone whispered to me that the chairs at the table were reserved for "the bigwigs," and that I should sit in the back with the other interns. Luckily, I didn't make that misstep in front of too many people, or I would have been embarrassed.

Be humble. Acknowledge your lack of experience and training. Remember, you're an intern, not a seasoned professional. It's okay to be unsure of yourself, but it's not okay to pretend to be more confident than you really are. Some students try to cover up their fears and insecurities with false bluster. A supervisor and coworkers will more readily respect true humility than grandiose overconfidence. Humility demonstrates that you're teachable and cooperative, whereas the person who comes in with a "know-it-all" attitude can be perceived as being difficult.

> Quick Tip: If you're really nervous and your hands are shaking, you might want to pass on the soft drink or cup of coffee that's offered to you. It wouldn't be the end of the world if you spilled it all over yourself or someone else, but why take the chance?

SAFETY

One of your first concerns should be your personal safety as well as the safety of those around you. Insofar as possible, do advance preparation and ask questions ahead of time. Be aware of your surroundings. You should know something about the neighborhood where you're assigned. Are there safety issues to be aware of, such as night-time activity, drug-dealing, violence? Ask where you should park, if you drove to the agency, and find out if you need an escort in or out of the building, particularly after dark. Many agencies are located in areas that may see a higher rate of street crime and violence. Just because you are a social worker there to do good does not protect you from crime in the area.

Assess the climate of your placement. Remember that not every person who walks into your agency is necessarily an innocent person there for help. It is possible that some may be there to help themselves to your purse or wallet. If you carry a purse or bag, either keep it with you at all times, or ask where it can be securely placed while you are on duty.

With many agencies, there may be a risk factor for potential violence directed toward you from clients, or even family members of clients. You may feel your client would never hurt you because you have a good relationship but that does not mean family members or friends have warm feelings toward you. In fact they may perceive you as a scapegoat, that you have somehow directly or indirectly caused problems for a client.

Some clients are voluntary, meaning they come to the agency by their choice, while others may be mandated by court orders, including treatment or jail mandates. Still others may have found services forced on them by agencies designed to protect the public, like child or adult protective agencies.

Persons in these situations may not experience you as a positive presence in their lives.

There is often a false sense of security in new interns: They believe they are somehow magically protected from harm from others because social workers do good things in the world. How could anyone be angry or violent toward us when we are there to do good? In fact, that feeling of being a do-gooder can cause you to be less vigilant, thereby increasing your chances of being a victim of violent actions. You need to recognize that we live in a society in which violence in general and in the workplace has increased.

> I recall a group of clients on their way to nearby vending machines. I was in the hallway heading in that direction to interview another client. As the group of clients passed, a woman took a fisted swing at me, missing me only by an inch. I was lucky. I should have been more alert and seen that this woman was agitated and that her behavior was likely to spin out of control.

We all want to be seen as "the good guy," but the reality is that sometimes social work teams make decisions that are seen as negative or even catastrophic to our clients. Teams sometimes decide to hospitalize people, remove children from a home, and so on, so you may not always be seen as the helper you believe and know yourself to be.

In some agencies, there may even be a possibility of violence between coworkers. It is likely that you will work with many different kinds of professionals, paraprofessionals, and nonskilled workers. Often there are conflicts, and it is not unheard of that a scuffle occurs. Your job is to be alert to anger, rage, and the possibility of tempers flaring out of control. In addition, it is not your responsibility to try to stop an argument or fight, but to quietly disappear and bring help. You are not exempt from violence because you are "the student."

Many agencies have strict dress code requirements related to safety. Specifically, you may find that high heels and slick-soled shoes are prohibited, along with anything worn around the neck that might leave the wearer vulnerable to choking. Dangling earrings, attention-getting jewelry, and suggestive clothing are also often banned.

At the first meeting with your supervisor, ask about:

> Staff experiences in the neighborhood
> Where to park
> Dress code (what and what not to wear for safety)
> Risks with your client population
> The agency's experience with violence in the building
> The home visit policy and staff experiences
> Agency training to handle aggressive and violent situations
> Training available to you as a student

Avoid trouble by monitoring your environment and staying out of difficult situations. Prevention is an important policy to follow. If you sense trouble brewing, probably the best thing you can do is to quietly bring help. Do not attempt to intervene in arguments, fistfights, or in any situation that seems to be "heating up."

Another way you can increase your personal safety is to help clients to feel safe with you. Do not aggressively confront, threaten, or otherwise back a client into a corner, either physically or verbally. Always allow them to keep their self-esteem and self-respect intact. Allow them a way to interpret situations in nonthreatening ways. Remember to "buy time" by temporarily smoothing situations over. You can get to the root of a problem later after consultation with your supervisor. Ask for any kind of help you need and don't be afraid to apologize or back down in a sticky situation.

SAFETY RULES

Some of this material was mentioned in an earlier chapter under agency rules, but your safety may depend on it, so let's review some of the rules before moving on to other topics. I want to remind you about different codes to alert staff to situations. I was in a meeting recently where it was mentioned that a seasoned employee did not know the emergency codes of the hospital. Do not find yourself in this situation! Ask if there are any code systems. Often you will find a color system such as code blue for a medical emergency. Or you may find the agency uses a phrase, such as "Dr. Redstone please come to office" to signal that an emergency is taking place. Other agencies will not have developed systems because of what they do or their size. However, that does not excuse you from asking your supervisor what to do in an emergency.

Similarly, find out the agency's policy on home visits to clients and transporting clients in vehicles. Veteran social workers have found themselves in volatile situations resulting in policy changes in their agencies. The home visit policy can vary. Some have you going alone while others have you traveling in pairs. Some require that the police meet you at the home depending on the nature of the home visit. The policy for transporting clients can also vary: you may be using your own vehicle or using only agency vehicles, and having more than one agency staff person accompany the client is often a requirement. The wide range of practices reflects the wide range of agencies and the differing views of staff responsibility. You need to know the policy of your agency; if you have concerns in a situation, discuss it with your supervisor.

A student asked if she could discuss her recent home visit experience. She had been on many home visits by herself and was very comfortable with this model. She went on a routine home visit to one of her clients. When she got there the client had been drinking, was hostile, and verbally threatening to her. She left immediately, returning to the agency and reporting the matter to her supervisor.

This was an emotionally charged event that required processing even after she had processed it with her supervisor. The lesson learned here is that circumstances can change, and that each home visit must be treated as potentially problematic. Be prepared to act, to protect yourself, and the safety of your client. A home visit to a friendly elderly women can change suddenly because a family member has dropped by to visit. I remind you that, as a social worker, you may have to do tasks that your client or the client's family may interpret as a threat. Examples would be a placement in an agency concerned with child protection, foster care placement, probation, or court-ordered treatment. You can easily see how in such contexts you may not be seen as the helpful social worker. Whatever agency you are placed in, you need to learn the policies and discuss these issues with your supervisor.

Never go on a home visit or have face to face contact with family members without the knowledge of your supervisor at your agency.

HEALTH PRECAUTIONS

You may be working with a client population often referred to as "at-risk" or "high risk." Whatever term is used in your agency, you must have a full understanding of what it means in relation to the clients you will serve. I want to highlight this point for your safety with clients in general. When we take a first-aid class, they discuss universal precautions—treating all people, and their body fluids, as if they are infected and taking the necessary precautions (gloves, mask, etc.)—to ensure you are not infected. If you take a CPR class, they will discuss universal precautions, because of Acquired Immune Deficiency Syndrome (AIDS). This topic may be adequately covered in your classroom but in the field we often do not think in universal precautions terms. Discuss the various risk factors that apply to your placement with your supervisor and develop a good working knowledge of these risks. Remember, knowledge is power. Develop an understanding of how AIDS is transmitted, you do not want to be fearful in your placement because you have been asked to work with a gay man or an IV drug user, both of whom may or may not be HIV positive. Someone you would never suspect may also be HIV positive. Therefore, use universal precautions at all times.

The populations that we serve are often multidimensional in their problems. For example, a homeless individual may also have health problems such as tuberculosis or hepatitis. Again, I emphasize, get a good understanding of the population in your placement agency. There are more examples that I could provide, but I believe I have made the point that you want to work comfortably with the clients in your placement and you need to feel safe through knowledge of your population. In these cases, ignorance is not bliss.

FAMILY CONTACT: APPROPRIATE AND INAPPROPRIATE

In conjunction with knowing your clients' health issues, you will need to know under what circumstances those issues, and other client issues, can be released or discussed with others. It is especially critical to know what you can and cannot discuss with family members. First, get to know the agency policy concerning contact with families. The rules of confidentiality in the medical field have been getting a good deal of attention recently with the passage of the Health Insurance Portability and Accountability Act, or HIPAA. HIPAA is a federal law that provides for the transfer of insurance benefits when changing employers or insurance companies. This has impacted the rules covering confidentiality because, in order to efficiently transfer insurance coverage, the companies need to exchange medical information efficiently. HIPAA defines what information can be exchanged with and without consent and how it can be exchanged. Despite the passing of this federal law, there is a great deal of difference in how individual agencies have interpreted its guidelines. You must check with your supervisor to determine what your agency policy is and how it is to be carried out.

SEXUAL HARASSMENT AND CULTURAL SENSITIVITY

Many agencies offer training in these two areas. Small agencies often send their staff to training seminars conducted by other trained professionals or invite specialists to their agency to train staff. Your college may have provided you with some basic knowledge on the subject of sexual harassment as part of freshman orientation. If you are given an opportunity to attend sexual harassment training or cultural sensitivity training, consider it a gift.

Because most of you have not had an opportunity to attend a training session, I will discuss them now. These seminars are often a four-hour, half-day training session, and my discussion of the topic is superficial. If you are in a situation where you are addressed in a manner that makes you feel uncomfortable, or if you are told a risqué joke that makes you feel uncomfortable, you may have just experienced sexual harassment. Starting at the end of the conversation, most jokes are discriminatory against some group: blonds, the elderly, and Polish people, for example. These kinds of jokes perpetuate a stereotyped image of a certain group, one that is generally negative. If you are a member of one of these groups, and a joke is told to you, how do you respond to the joke teller?

Any time you feel you are in a situation that makes you feel uncomfortable, you need to seek support. The first line of support is your on-site supervisor. If it is not a day you would normally speak to your supervisor, indicate that it is important. The second line of support is your field work faculty. This may be necessary if the person making you feel uncomfortable is your on-site supervisor. What you don't want to do is nothing! Most large agencies have policies and procedures to follow in such situations, but even in small settings this type of behavior is not acceptable and needs to be reported.

SOCIAL WORK ETHICS AND VALUES

More than likely, you were attracted to the field of social work, at least partially, because your personal values are the same as those of other social workers. Throughout history, social work values have remained consistent. The Code of Ethics of the National Association of Social Workers is based on the six core values of social work:

- Service ("Social workers' primary goal is to help people in need and to address social problems.")
- Social justice ("Social workers challenge social injustice.")
- Dignity and worth of the person ("Social workers respect the inherent dignity and worth of the person.")
- Importance of human relationships ("Social workers recognize the central importance of human relationships.")
- Integrity ("Social workers behave in a trustworthy manner.")
- Competence ("Social workers practice within their areas of competence and develop and enhance their professional expertise.")

You may want to post these values above your desk or in a prominent place so they can inspire and inform you in your daily activities. It can be helpful to read and review these values often.

RESOURCES IN DEALING
WITH ETHICAL ISSUES

When you are faced with an ethical dilemma or uncertainty about your course of action, many resources are available to you. Of course, you will first consult with your supervisor about any ethical dilemmas you experience.

You may also want to discuss these issues with your peers and perhaps with selected coworkers, or it could provide material for in-class discussions. It could happen that the college discussion, in class, and the agency see the situation differently. Do not get in the middle if this occurs; your faculty supervisor will take the lead if necessary.

In addition to seeking supervision, the following resources are also available.

1. NASW Code of Ethics. You should already be very familiar with the social work code of ethics. Hopefully, you have studied and discussed it thoroughly with your professors. Now it is your chance to put these principles to work on a daily basis. Keep a copy of the code of ethics handy so you can consult it whenever you have doubts about what you should or should not do.

2. Another great resource for both you and your supervisor is the NASW Office of Ethics and Professional Review. As a student member of the National Association of Social Workers, you may consult by telephone with a representative of the NASW who can offer ethical advice on a toll-free line.

3. Additionally, NASW's Web site offers an "ethical dilemma of the month." In this feature, composites of member's ethical issues are posted, along with a response indicating which section or sections of the NASW Code of Ethics may apply to the issue. Questions for thought and discussion are also posted in order to help you make good ethical decisions.

4. Many textbooks and videos about ethics in social work are available.

5. Some states have Web sites, such as New York state under the Commissioner for the Quality of Care for the Mentally Disabled, www.cqc.ny. state.us.

ETHICS AND ETHICAL THINKING

As social workers, we have a code of ethics that all of us in the profession share. Textbooks in the field make reference to the National Association of Social Workers (NASW) Code of Ethics. This code is your foundation for ethical behavior, but that is not the end of the story.

You have discussed the code in your classroom work, but now let's focus on how the code translates to the field. You must know the rules of your agency. Are you allowed to talk to other workers about a case, or can you speak to only certain individuals? Are you allowed to discuss your client with another agency; what is the policy; do you need a release of information? Don't assume, ask!

> Please don't talk about your client in the hallways. You will hear such conversations all the time, but it is a not good practice and likely violates the confidentiality policies of your agency.

In your internship, you may encounter a variety of ethical dilemmas:

- When your clients have violated their probation, are you obligated to tell the parole officer, or is this information confidential?
- If your client has a history of setting fires and is ready for placement, will you be expected to downplay this history so as to avoid rejection from the new placement?
- If your client is under age and tells you about behaviors that may be dangerous, do you tell the parents?
- If your client is HIV positive and is engaging in unprotected sex with someone you may even know, should you warn that individual?
- If your client tells you in conversation of a situation that suggests neglect or abuse, what do you do?

Each situation has its own ethical issues that arise out of the concerns and rights of the individual you are working with and the rights of others. When ethical situations appear to be a mine field, seek the support of your supervisor. Stay on solid ground.

First, always treat your clients with respect and dignity. Second, demonstrate good social work values and ethical behavior by following the code of ethics. Third, review the agency code of ethics, which can be found in the policy and procedures manual. Fourth, when in doubt, go to your supervisor or someone in the agency who can help. Do not act on your own without consultation from an authoritative source. Remember that you, too, have rights, values, and ethical standards that may also come into play in any ethical situation. Your personal rights and values may collide with your agency's policies or assignments. What happens when you do not agree with what you are told? Again, see your supervisor for support and your college/university faculty to guide you.

The NASW Code of Ethics concerns social workers' ethical responsibilities to clients, to colleagues, in practice settings, as professionals, to the social work profession, and to society as a whole.

To clients: Remember that you are your clients' advocate, and that you must treat each client (and family) with the utmost respect. That respect must be extended not only to the client personally, but in your written materials, and when talking with colleagues about a client. If you have problems respecting a particular client, discuss the matter with your supervisor, because attitudes you may think are hidden could "leak out" in your speech, manner, or bearing. If you have conflicts with a client, this issue becomes important "material" for supervisory sessions.

Confidentiality: One of the most important ethical issues regarding clients has to do with confidentiality. When do you discuss clients' rights and issues of confidentiality with your clients? Do you do it at the beginning when you first meet the clients, and are you knowledgeable enough to discuss it with your client at this point in your learning experience? What will happen if you explain it poorly? Will the client feel trust in you and are you then put in a situation where you feel you need to share information with others, but are not sure you explained the policy correctly to the client?

We are all learning the ins and outs of the new Health Information Portability and Accountability Act, better known to us as HIPAA. This act has had an important impact on the providers of services and you as a social worker. This new law affects everything from faxes sent to letters mailed that contain a client's health information. The agency where you are interning has addressed the new HIPAA law and will explain to you their guidelines. There are some broad issues I will discuss now. First is the concept of Protected Health Information (PHI). Basically, any information about a client that the agency maintains in the context of the medical care provided by the agency falls under the definition of PHI, and, as such, is covered under the confidentiality statutes of the law. This includes very basic information like the identity of your clients. You will see letters and packets labeled "PHI confidential: to be opened by addressee only" on a good deal of the mail sent out of your agency. In the past, a common way to send client information would be to write "confidential" on the envelope. The important thing to remember is that client information is confidential and needs to be protected. The agency where you are doing your placement will show you the guidelines they use.

The second general issue is that of disclosure of information. The agency has a responsibility to track all disclosures of information for each client. This is often done on a form kept in the client record. What is or is not a disclosure needs to be discussed at your agency for clarification. Take notes. Don't just rely on your memory when you discuss this topic. Your placement agency will give you much more information on this topic that you will need to understand. As always, ask for help from your supervisor if you have questions.

You can find more information on the Web on this topic and you have already been exposed to HIPAA policy at your drugstore and doctor's office. Be proactive—get a copy of the HIPAA policy handed out at your agency.

With this new information, let's see how this student handles the topic of confidentiality in her process recording:

HE SAID/SHE SAID	SUPERVISOR COMMENTS
W: I want to go over confidentiality, do you know what that means?	
D: Yeah you can't take my chart or information without my permission.	
W: Yes, there is more, what you say stays between me and you, unless you are going to harm yourself or others. I am obligated to tell my supervisor (I wasn't sure . . .)	Not really true, you tell all in this process recording.

This is a good example of a student's dilemma. The college is talking about the rules of confidentiality and student supervisors are discussing it at the agency. The student had no place to go but to put the issue on the table with the client as best as she could. Be aware there are many pressures on you to perform, including your own internal pressures. There are the written client rights and within that, what and how client confidentiality is described. Then there is the assumed confidentiality, working in a team setting, and with your on-site supervisor.

The written institutional procedures to protect clients' rights to confidentiality should be there at your work location in a policy manual. Ask to see it even if you feel the supervisor has explained it and you feel you have a full and complete understanding of the concept and how it works. Do not think you know the agency's policies because of personal experience or because you have read your discipline's code of ethics. Each agency has its own rules concerning confidentiality. If these rules are not spelled out clearly in the agency manual, then ask for clarity on the subject from your agency supports, generally your supervisor.

Many agencies work as a team, and information about clients is shared with all members of the team. This setup creates a more complex situation concerning what can and should be shared. Information shared can range from "broad strokes" of a client's life to specific and detailed situations.

If you work in an agency that treats clients with medication, what is your responsibility to share information with doctors so they can give the best possible care? Who has access to the client's records and how and where is the information collected?

A client of mine reported that he is thinking about starting to drink again, and he is concerned because drinking has gotten him into a lot of trouble in the past. He also told me he lies awake at night and imagines having a sexual relationship with an attractive female in his therapy group.

What is important to share with a team is the concern that the client may drink again and the impact that action may have for that person. If other members of the team are interacting with this client, this is the type of information that needs to be shared. If you feel there is any danger to another client, then you need to talk with the team, and know your agency's policies along with your state's laws concerning warning a person in danger.

Remember to discriminate between what is interesting or of shock value versus what is actually important.

In team meeting one day, I observed that a male client had started plucking his eyebrows. Immediately following the meeting, a team member confronted the client, backing him against a wall and demanding to know if he was a homosexual or not. The client became agitated, upset, and seemed to be doing poorly for several weeks. From that time on, I was more careful about the kinds of information I relayed to that particular member of the team.

A simple rule of thumb will help: Will the issue or event you are planning to disclose help the client in some way? Help should not be a narrow view of only relating positive things, but includes negatives as well. For example, telling someone that your client is drinking a six pack of beer a day is a negative disclosure, but without that information, medications may be impacted and treatment will not be addressed to the entire situation.

Access to records: Due to the changes in various state and federal laws, clients now have greater access to their medical or agency records than ever before. Be informed about the laws in your state, and ask your supervisor about your responsibilities in making records available to clients. This availability will likely influence what you might write in progress reports or chart notes.

Relationships: Sexual relationships with current or former clients are unethical. In addition, the code of ethics states: "Providing clinical services to a former sexual partner has the potential to be harmful to the individual and is likely to make it difficult for the social worker and individual to maintain appropriate professional boundaries." Be sure you know both the material relating to appropriate physical contact with clients and clear boundary setting. Of course, any form of sexual harassment is off limits.

Social relationships with clients or clients' family members are also not permitted. If you live in a small town, for example, there may be sticky issues involved if you already know the client even slightly, attend the same school, church, or synagogue. Additionally, if you keep "bumping into" a client, that can be uncomfortable for you as well as for your client. Check with your supervisor for his or her expectations in this regard. Will you be expected to pretend you don't know your client if you accidentally meet in a social situation? At what point will you be expected to speak up and tell your supervisor that you cannot work with a particular client because you are too close to that person to be objective?

ETHICAL BEHAVIOR TOWARD COLLEAGUES

What does it mean to behave ethically toward colleagues? The concept of respect is paramount. Use the "Golden Rule," and treat your coworkers as you would like to be treated. This means no gossip, no backbiting, and so on. Make an honest effort to cooperate and be a good team member, even though you may not like or even respect all your colleagues. Remember that you have come from an idealistic perspective into the real world, which you may find to be different than you expected it to be. You may find that you question the maturity and ethical behavior of some of your colleagues when they do not behave perfectly. Remember that everyone is human, and we all have our bad days. Some of us have personal or professional problems that creep into dealings with others. It will be helpful if you can give your colleagues the benefit of the doubt and interpret their behavior in the most positive light possible for as long as possible.

Never assume people are acting maliciously, when their behavior may be actually due to ignorance, lack of education, hardship, mental or physical illness, deprivation, fatigue, or a misguided attempt to relieve their own pain by lashing out.

ETHICS DEMYSTIFIED

The National Association of Social Workers' Code of Ethics can be a bit overwhelming for both experienced and novice social workers. In their book, *Delivering Health Care in America* (1979), Shi and Singh do an excellent job of looking at the basic elements.

They refer to four principles that may help you understand this important issue: respect for others, beneficence, nonmalfeasance, and justice. Respect for others has four subcomponents: autonomy, truth-telling, confidentiality, and fidelity. First, autonomy refers to the clients' right to make decisions for themselves, because they are partners in the planning of treatment: they give consent and make choices without coercion. If you have ever been a patient in a hospital, you will understand how patients often feel they are at the mercy of the caregivers. This is an area where professionals often have difficulty, feeling they are the experts and neglecting to include the client in the treatment decisions. The second part, truth-telling, simply means that you are honest with your client. If your client asks questions and you don't know the answers, don't guess, but try to find answers. Faking answers will not encourage a trusting relationship. The third is confidentiality of information. It is your duty to protect information about your client from third parties. Be sure to discuss HIPAA with your supervisor. However, often you will work as a team and when you have a supervisor you share information about your work. This is clearly allowed by HIPAA (Health Information Portability and Accountability Act). The fourth component is fidelity: keep your word and behave in a professional manner. This can refer to anything: the time and day you will meet your client, rescheduling in advance when necessary, and keeping your word if you say you are going to fill out those forms or make that call. Also, you have introduced yourself as the social work student or social work intern; that defines your role and your duties. In fact, you may have clarified your role in your first meeting with the client.

Beneficence simply means that, as you enter into the client–worker relationship, you undertake to do all you can to alleviate pain and suffering. You may think this applies more to the medical profession, but there are all types of suffering. Going hand-and-hand with beneficence is non-malfeasance. Simply put, your moral obligation is to do no harm. Again, this is not only an issue for doctors, but also for social workers. The interventions you make should, to the best of your ability, not cause harm to your client. The final element of ethical behavior is justice. You should treat your client with fairness and be nondiscriminatory, which at times can be difficult.

You will find embedded in your agency code of ethics these simple but relevant four basic principles. They are to be valued and should be part of your values as a social worker.

Ask: Don't assume you already know the answer. Remember: The only dumb questions are the ones you didn't ask.

In terms of the decision-making process, the ethical issues you will confront in the field are not that different from those that wind up in the ethics committee of your university. You will find that, in a general hospital setting, the ethics committee will meet as often as necessary, often dealing with life-and-death issues. Other institutions have monthly or even bimonthly meetings. Membership should include a wide range of professional disciplines and laypeople. You will find, however, that this varies from agency to agency. Some agencies are very small and do not have the support of an ethics committee to examine issues. Even if that is the case at your agency, you are still bound by the code of ethics of your discipline. If you feel you are in an ethical dilemma, ask your supervisor what the procedure is for dealing with the issue.

> Recently, a student approached me and was very concerned with events that had taken place at his agency related to his client. This was a small agency that often dealt with the court system. In this situation there was no ethics committee. After discussions with his supervisor, the matter was brought to his faculty supervisor. It was also the subject of a classroom discussion. The matter was resolved, but only because of the student's persistence. The point is that it is your responsibility to not rest until you are satisfied that the ethical dilemma you face is addressed.

Not all ethical situations are going to be resolved to your satisfaction and you may be left with many confusing feelings. It is important to share this with your supervisor and your facility's supervisor of placements. You need to process the feelings and grow from the experience.

Below is an outline that highlights points you will need to address when confronted with an ethical dilemma. You can find some form of this outline in any generalist book on social work.

ETHICAL DECISION PROCESS

- Write down the ethical problem or issue.
- Who is involved? Make a list, think micro, mezzo, and macro.
- Review ethical standards: Do the issues present an ethical dilemma?
- Present ethical dilemma to the treatment team, supervisor, or others; include your role/investment.
- Reevaluate the situation for significance of the ethical issue. Continue or discontinue discussion.
- What is your conclusion? (Does your supervisor support your decision?)

SURVEYS, RESEARCH, AND THE INSTITUTIONAL REVIEW BOARD (IRB)

Institutional Review Boards (IRB) are part of the process an agency must participate in if research is to be done at an agency. IRBs are composed of a group of individuals, often appointed, that reviews all proposed research in order to protect the agency clientele from exploitation. In many ways they represent the social morals of the agency by protecting the clients from frivolous research. They look to ensure that the research being conducted is for the betterment of the clients. An IRB completes its function by reviewing submitted applications from researchers. The researchers must provide the IRB with a good deal of information, such as the population (clients) involved in the research project, who will do the research, and a clear, worthwhile purpose demonstrating how this will benefit the population. (This is a gross oversimplification; even the application can be overwhelming.)

What does all this have to do with you? Possibly, one of your assignments from class may involve doing surveys or questionnaires at your agency. You may be doing an organizational change project or learning how to evaluate a program's effectiveness. Often you will need the approval of an IRB to distribute your questionnaire or survey. Your college may have an IRB process that you must report to prior to doing any research in the agency and you may need approval from the agency's IRB. Speak to your supervisor about this, to be sure you understand you meet all the necessary requirements. You do not want to find your in-class assignment incomplete because you failed to follow the agency rules.

Remember, there are several ways to do research: observations, surveys, experiments, and archival review. All need the approval of an IRB. Archival review, as a rule, will require less documentation in the application because you will not be working directly with clients.

NOTES TO YOURSELF

Reminders of things to do: _____

_____

_____

_____

_____

_____

_____

_____

Situations that relate to readings: _____

_____

_____

_____

_____

_____

_____

_____

Questions to ask your supervisor: _____

_____

_____

_____

_____

_____

_____

_____

Supervisor's comments: _____

_____

_____

_____

_____

_____

_____

_____

■ ■ ■ ■ ■ ▬▬▬▬▬▬▬▬▬▬▬▬▬▬▬▬▬▬▬▬▬▬▬▬▬▬▬▬▬▬

CHAPTER 4

STAYING THE COURSE

A large part of being successful in a field placement has to do with settling in for the long haul and getting comfortable with day-to-day routines of your agency. In truth, you will probably never get as comfortable as the social workers employed at your agency, for several reasons: You're being evaluated by at least two people, your supervisor and the teacher of the course at your school, so you may feel that you are under scrutiny during your entire placement. You're also walking in as "the new kid on the block," and, for a while at least, all eyes will be on you. Once you seem to be fitting in, things will relax a bit, you'll feel more comfortable, and everything will settle down to something of a routine. It may seem that, just as you're getting the hang of everything, your placement will be finished, and you'll be on to the next chapter in your life.

THE TEAM AND AGENCY AS SYSTEMS

In the classroom you have defined and discussed micro, mezzo, and macro theories of practice. You are now experiencing all three at the same time and you may not fully realize the process until it is pointed out to you. Any agency you are assigned to is a system and system issues will be present. Large institutions may make it easier to see the systems issues on all three levels, departments, wards, or specialty units within the institution. A classic example would be a general hospital, but social work placements are in small agencies as well. It may be harder to see the systems issues at all three levels, but they are there. Become aware of the three levels within your agency, and you will understand why things change and why they do not change. Listen intently at team meetings or department meetings, learn the issues, and identify the problems. Remember there are many combinations, so be alert. Here are some possibilities: There is the team (often multidisciplined), the client group, the social work department, the agency as part of a larger organization. Another combination is you, your supervisor, and your clients. Funding sources are also part of the system; do not ignore them.

If you are called on to identify the micro, mezzo, and macro systems in your placement, one tool that may help you get started is drawing an ecosystem. By placing you, your client, or your agency in the center you can identify the surrounding elements and their impact on the central figure.

MULTICULTURAL INTERVIEW

Before you engage a client in your first interview or an assessment process, you need to have a solid understanding that your client may belong to a different culture than your own. Many agencies involve the staff in cultural diversity training, not to be used for work with clients, but for working with diverse cultural groups among the staff. Their efforts are to increase awareness, sensitivity, and understanding that different cultures may not interpret a situation in the same way. This is not the same as your classroom discussion about understanding cultural diversity and the multicultural interview. You must be aware that the clients you will be helping can and will bring a varied range of cultural differences. Your sensitivity to this is essential in the helping process. You do not want to make interventions that are inappropriate and useless for this individual because you did not take the time to understand the client's culture. Yes, it is true that clients are very forgiving if you make a mistake and will give you a second chance, but that does not excuse you the second time, and really not even the first time if you did your homework.

Always begin with the basics: Treat your client as an individual, with respect and dignity. Do not assume you understand a culture because you have read material about it. Within cultures there are wide ranges of variation. Look at your own culture and see the diversity and similarities you experience with others of the same culture, in terms of behaviors, traditions, values, and attitudes.

- Take time to understand the client's culture.
- Ask clients about their culture when appropriate.
- Ask your supervisor about agency experience with specific cultures.
- Find reading material relevant to the client's ethnicity.
- Learn the cultural taboos.
- Learn the cultural behaviors.
- Be aware there is verbal as well as nonverbal communication.

There are enough pitfalls in building a trusting relationship with a client, and errors concerning cultural differences are avoidable if you take the time to do your homework.

ASSESSMENTS

Assessments are critical tools in social work, and your understanding of them is important. There are many types of assessments, all with the same intent: to gather information on clients. The range is enormous, including developmental history, mental status, family history, vocational history, and medical history, just to name a few. These assessments are known by many different names, often depending on the agency where you are. So the first order of business is to familiarize yourself with the assessments your placement uses. Ask for copies of blank forms so you can review and look for areas you don't fully understand. You can then discuss these with your supervisor.

Perhaps one of the best ways you can serve your client is to be generally familiar with the bio-psychosocial model of assessment or comprehensive client history. Look for strengths and weakness in your clients. Use this information to build your assessment. Some agencies will be very narrow in their focus, others will not be, so follow the lead of your placement.

> The mental status assessment I learned in one agency is of little use to me in my current graduate school placement. My new supervisor concentrates on my assessment of the clients' needs, but is not very interested in the clients' moods, for example. I'm glad I learned that particular assessment, even though it's not valuable to me right now. I'm happy I was able to build a broad base of assessment knowledge that may come in handy later on in my career as I become more specialized.

Assessment skills may be in use, even when they don't appear to be.

> I was visiting my mother in the hospital following her surgery and in the next bed was a patient who had just received a lung transplant. One of the hospital's social workers came to meet with this patient to discuss and review insurance coverage for post-hospital care. The bulk of the time was spent discussing what benefits the patient qualified for at this time. Seems narrow in focus, yes, but the role of this social worker was to assist the client with managing financially with life-long medications. That does not mean that, at the same time, the social worker was not assessing the client in terms of acceptance of the new organ and the life changes the client will be making, the impact on family, or the ability to work.

Assessments can be carried out in many ways, and the more skilled you become, the less mechanical and obvious the process will be. In your assessment of an individual, you will identify that person's strengths and weaknesses. The terms may be labeled differently, but the concepts remain the same. Remember that a strength can also be a weakness and vice-versa. For example, although a client has an intact family (a strength), there may be constant arguments (a weakness), thus causing a high level of stress for the client. So let's review:

1. Find out what assessment tools your placement uses.
2. Make copies and become familiar with them.
3. Understand that assessments have many names and functions, depending on the agency.
4. Always look for client strengths in doing assessments.
5. Be aware that you may be called on to assess your client for substance abuse, physical or sexual abuse, and dangerousness to self or others. Always look to your supervisor for guidance in this area. If your supervisor is not available, see another professional before your client leaves the agency.

Generalist Practice

There are two basic assessments that you have surely learned along the way, the genogram and an eco-map. Ashman and Hull do a nice job of explaining the two concepts in *Understanding Generalist Practice* (2002), as do Johnson and Yanca in *Social Work Practice* (1998). If your placement agency does not have resource books on assessments that cover many types, an economical book to purchase is Susan Lukas's *Where to Start and What to Ask* (1993).

A word of caution: Use the assessments your field placement agency approves. Always ask your supervisor about using any tool that is not included in agency policy.

Eco-Map.   An eco-map is an excellent tool for looking at the social forces that impact on a person, family, or even a system, but it is not a tool to be used in all situations. If you are not familiar with this tool, the circles in Figure 4.1 are the persons, family members, or agencies, and the arrows are the direction of the forces.

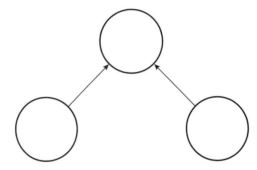

Genogram.   A genogram, shown in Figure 4.2, is an excellent tool to get clients involved in the work. Do the drawing with them. As they begin to understand the rules, they will often volunteer information. It is a good tool for relaxing clients and building a relationship with them. The method is simple:

- boxes for males
- circles for females
- an "X" through a box indicates a death
- solid lines indicate a relationship
- dotted lines mean a less formal relationship
- a slash in a line indicates a separation of some type

Label items as needed, such as the date of a death, or an important anniversary date.

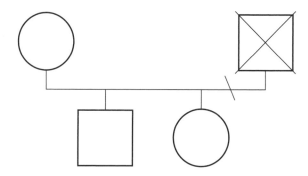

This genogram indicates that a couple was divorced and the children are with the mother. Notice the location of the slash. The date can be put on the line. A dotted line, rather than a slash, would indicate a separation. The X through the father means he is deceased. Here, too, a date can be added.

Psychiatric Assessment

It is unlikely you will be called on to do a psychiatric assessment, but I wanted to mention it as a tool for advocating on behalf of a client regarding medication issues. A mental status exam is a snapshot in time of the individual you are working with. Your ability to communicate a client's mental status to the doctor will help him or her determine if the client needs to be evaluated. I am giving you an overview of what is included; speak to your supervisor for more details.

- How is he or she dressed? Is it appropriate for the season and situation?
- What is the client's mood?
- What is the client's affect: Does his or her affect match his or her mood? Is there a full range of expression?
- How is the rate of speech: slow/deliberate/average?
- What is the tone: soft/loud/average?
- How is the content of the speech: appropriate to questions and conversation?
- Are there any symptoms of suicidal thoughts, or a plan to harm him- or herself?
- Are there any symptoms of homicidal thoughts, or a plan to harm someone else?
- What is the client's ability to process ideas?
- How is the client's perception of situations?

- Are there any illusions or hallucinations?
- How good is his or her cognitive ability? Is he or she oriented in three spheres—time, place, and person?
- How good is his or her memory, both recent and remote?

At first you may find the questions difficult to understand. If you are in a placement where psychiatric assessments are done, your supervisor can help you better understand the questions. You can see by the list of questions that these are not the typical social work questions you would be asking. However, an awareness of these questions and how they relate to your client may make you a better advocate on that client's behalf. Additional questions can address the past psychiatric history, history of treatment, and any history of drug or alcohol use/abuse.

> A former student called to give me an update on her placement in graduate school. She remarked that her superior was not interested in her ability to do a mental status on her current cases, but she found it a valuable tool nonetheless.

Psychosocial Assessment

As social work students you are already familiar with taking the history of a client from your classroom work. I strongly suggest that you role-play asking the questions with a fellow student. Rehearsing will only make you better. Because you are already familiar with a psychosocial history, I will not detail the task, but instead focus on several areas often overlooked: sexual abuse as a victim or abuser, high-risk behavior such as sexual activity, including HIV status, and substance abuse. Questions to ask about sexual behavior:

- Has anyone ever touched you in any way that caused you to feel ashamed or uncomfortable?
- Has this happened more than once and/or with more than one person?
- Have you ever been a victim of a violent crime?
- Did you ever witness a violent crime or suicide attempt?
- If so, was this a traumatic experience, and has it affected your life, either your behavior, feelings, or thoughts?
- Have you ever spoken to someone professionally in relation to the feelings or thoughts?
- When you first became sexually active, was it consensual?
- At what age did you become sexually active?
- Are you currently sexually active?
- Have you used any form of protective barrier during sexual relations, now or in the past?
- Have you ever been tested for HIV?
- What led you to get HIV testing?

Questions to ask related to alcohol/drug use and abuse:

- Do you currently use alcohol or illegal substances?
- What is the substance? How often and how much do you use?
- Do you believe you have ever been impaired physically or psychologically due to use?
- Have you or someone else ever suggested you have a problem with this substance?
- Have you ever been in treatment for substance abuse, including alcohol?

These few questions are the tip of the iceberg. Many agencies have an assessment form you can use for the evaluation of substance use and abuse. If not, ask your supervisor to direct you to appropriate material.

Assessments, when done properly, are time-consuming, but yield a wealth of information. The assessment questions listed here are only a few of the possible assessment questions.

Assessing Potential for Violent Behavior

Your safety and the safety of your client is a critical area of practice experience and needs to be understood thoroughly. There are many assessment tools for assessing the presence and extent of danger to self or others. I review some of the basics to help you begin to develop a frame of reference. Your supervisor is the authority at your placement and matters that relate to this topic need to be thoroughly discussed with him or her.

Some states have laws that specify the actions you will need to take if an individual is assessed as dangerous to self or others. In the area of dangerousness to others, the California ruling is referred to as the Tarasoff ruling, based on a lawsuit wherein one of the parties was Tarasoff. You can access information regarding the Tarasoff ruling by doing a Web search.

Never let a client that you perceive as dangerous to self or others leave the office until you have spoken to your supervisor or another professional at the agency.

Some questions to consider asking to probe for a client's potential for violence:

- The best predictor of behavior is past behavior: Is there a history of violent behavior?
- Is there a history of abuse, physical or sexual?

- Is there history of risky behavior, such as drugs or alcohol?
- Is there a history of unpredictable behavior or impulsiveness?
- Does the person experience paranoia, now or in the past, such as perceiving you or others as wanting to harm him or her?
- Does the person have delusions or hallucinations? (Pay special attention to command hallucinations.)
- Is there a history of suicide attempts?
- When was the last time the client had suicidal feelings and how long has he or she felt this way?
- Are the means to carry out the act available to the client?

An assessment area that is often neglected is physical health. Remember, some psychological disorders are rooted in physical problems. There are many examples, but several classics include appearing drunk but really suffering from diabetes, appearing confused but really having a urinary tract infection (especially in the elderly), or appearing delusional or confused due to the cognitive difficulties associated with head trauma. When it is appropriate, and especially if your agency does not do one or deemphasizes physical issues, take a medical/physical history. You may be surprised by what you find.

GETTING COMFORTABLE WITH YOUR CLIENTS

Deep listening means that you are fully present with your client, that you are concentrating on both the content of what is being said as well as the underlying feelings. Deep listening is a way of listening "with the heart" and with understanding and empathy. You are not rehearsing what you are going to say next, you are simply getting a feel for what your client's emotional and mental worlds are like. A simple example of a session with a client in which the student felt comfortable in exploring new material follows.

Student feels stupid:

HE SAID/SHE SAID	SUPERVISORY COMMENTS
W: Not to switch subjects, but last week you spoke about your wife, I was wondering what made you get married at a young age, you were 21 and she was 19. (I wanted to get to know him more, more than just about his goals, who he was before his illness.)	You need to close old topic before changing to a new one.
C: No I was 19 and she was 21.	

W: Oh, that's right you were younger than her.
(I felt stupid because I forgot he told me)

You are allowed to be human

C: I was smoking a lot of reefer and I met her at her sister's house. I smoked with her.

Her meaning the sister?

W: So you got married because you were on drugs?

Was she using drugs? Did she think he would stop?

C: I can't say that.

W: So it was a common bond between you and her?
(Was that judgmental? I didn't mean to it to be.)

The following process recordings are examples of common situations students get themselves into early in their placement.

Professional student:

HE SAID/SHE SAID	SUPERVISORY COMMENTS
C: When I first come here the doctors said I was schizophrenic. I don't know if that was caused by smoking marijuana. What are you psychologist, psychiatrist? (Confused on why he got that assessment.)	
W: No, I'm a social work student but I can tell you what schizophrenia is. (He is looking interested. Nervous, I didn't want to mess up.)	
C: OK	
W: Schizophrenia is a disorder of the brain, the symptoms include . . .	Sounds very professional, put in layman's terms.

Don't get stuck in professional jargon. Don't talk down to your clients or above their heads. If in doubt, you can ask your clients if they understand and ask them to explain concepts in their own words.

Born leader:

HE SAID/SHE SAID	SUPERVISORY COMMENTS
W: It must be frustrating for you.	Leading
C: Yes, I was just talking about that to a friend of mine. I should be working or something now.	He got you hook, line, and sinker
W: It sounds like you are a little down.	
C: Sometimes I am, but I am working hard to change that.	
W: You are working hard at change. (Felt sad for him. Felt like I wanted to fix everything for him. I was trying to tune into him.)	Leading There is a difference—asking a feeling question to get validation

Trust your feelings: If you sense a client is feeling a certain way, ask! Don't fill in the blank for the client: you could be wrong. If you find your client is struggling for a word, you can make suggestions and give choices: "Are you feeling sad or blue or something else?"

Anxious student:

HE SAID/SHE SAID	SUPERVISORY COMMENTS
W: Before we stop and you make your call home, I want to ask you something.	Feeling unsure as to how things are going?
C: OK. After that I can make my phone call.	He will say anything to use the phone at this moment.
W: Yes, I want to ask, did you like the session that you and I had?	
C: Yes.	
W: Are there . . . topics that you would like to focus on?	This is where you begin the session.

How do you acquire good judgment? Good judgment comes only with experience. How do you get experience? Experience comes from making mistakes. Learn that your mistakes will help you mature in your skills as a social worker.

Looking beneath the Surface

We all carry "norms" in our minds that specify what is "normal" and what is not. Your norms have been shaped by your family, school, and the larger society around you. When you first look at the "outer picture" of a client, one of the questions you will ask yourself is whether or not the person seems "normal" to you. If the person is out of the ordinary, you might ask, "Is this person bizarre?" If so, what does the uniqueness mean? When you look at or listen to a client and "red flags" pop up in your mind, check your perceptions with others and discuss your feelings about what is happening with that particular person.

> One of our clients needed to be hospitalized from time to time. One of the first indicators that she was having difficulty coping was that she would begin to wear extreme, brightly colored makeup caked in layers on her face and arms. The first time I saw her in one of these phases, her appearance was so striking that, instantly, my inner radar sprang to life and the warning buzzers were set off in my head.

Look for the opposite beneath the behavior that sticks out. Rule of thumb: When someone's behavior, manner, or appearance is so extreme that it catches your attention, you might expect to find the opposite under the obvious behavior.

Student survives surprise:

HE SAID/SHE SAID	SUPERVISORY COMMENTS
W: You were in . . . hospital? How did you get to this hospital? Were you agitated with someone? (I read his chart and it said he was acting in a bizarre manner and irritated. Started to yell and point at me. He turned his chair around and sat sideways.)	Very confrontational start!!!
C: You calling me crazy? Do you think I am psycho?	Address behavior
W: I didn't say you were crazy. (I was a little nervous because I never had a client yell at me. I was trying not to be defensive but I made my point. I didn't mean to offend him.)	What did he hear you say? Good, be careful!
C: No, you implied it.	
W: How did I imply that?	

Continued

HE SAID/SHE SAID	SUPERVISORY COMMENTS
C: (starts to laugh/stops) I need a beer.	
(He has a history of alcohol abuse. I ignored the last topic because it overwhelmed me; my anxieties were up)	
W: When was the last time you had a beer?	Good question Topic change, can tell you were regrouping

Can you imagine what this student must have been feeling at that time? She handled the situation nicely for a first-year intern. However, the importance of the process recording is that you often don't know when a situation will become threatening. Ideally, this client would never have been assigned to the student if there had been any indication this would happen.

If you are endangered, who has the power to help you out of trouble? You may be surprised to learn that, at many agencies, the level of safety has a great deal to do with workers helping one another. For example, a janitor or secretary may have rapport with clients and be able to step in and "rescue" you from a difficult situation. For this reason, take pains to make friends with all the staff, not just the professionals. Chat with them; ask about their families; and don't think you're better than they are just because you've been to college and they haven't. Some workers resent students who give the appearance of acting superior to others. The truth is that often these students don't feel superior at all, but ill-at-ease, shy, or unsure of themselves and often come off as arrogant. Make sure no one gets that impression of you, and when you're in a crunch, you may find help coming from unexpected sources.

Understanding Your Client (Starting Where the Client Is)

If social work were a building and we were to name the cornerstones, one would surely be the phrase, "Start where the client is." This phrase sounds simple, but the process can be very complicated, even for a seasoned professional.

Student's first steps:

HE SAID/SHE SAID	SUPERVISORY COMMENTS
W: Hi D	
H: Hi	
W: I'll be your social worker. I'm a student. (Feel comfortable speaking to him.)	

D: You're not a worker?	Sounds like the client is concerned with
W: No, I am a social work	your qualifications.
intern. I'll be here until May.	Good comeback
D: OK	
W: I want to go over	Why did we start here, rather than
confidentiality, do you know	where the client is.
what that means?	

This process recording has a number of items but let's focus on the topic of knowing what the client's issue is. Here we see a student worried about getting in all the important things she was taught, especially issues of confidentiality. She did not give the client time to say why he was there. The student's qualifications were questioned as well but this was not addressed by the student. These are common mistakes students make early in their placement because they are anxious to do a good job and say all the right things.

Student wants it perfect:

HE SAID/SHE SAID	SUPERVISORY COMMENTS
W: Good morning. Thank you for meeting with me.	
C: (almost inaudible) Good morning.	
W: I guess I'll start by telling you about my role here.	
C: (nod)	
(I don't know what to say. I wanted to say the perfect thing to draw her out, knowing that it wasn't possible.)	
W: I am a social work student and that basically means that I have more time to meet with you because I have fewer clients. Have you ever worked with a student before?	Stop after who you are. This is true but would she care? What does it mean to her? Closed question
C: Yes.	
(I felt uncomfortable.)	

It is important that the client understand who you are and your role, so you must be clear about your role in the placement. This student demonstrated a clear understanding of her role. The next process recording is a student's first client in week one of the placement.

Student with sweating palms:

HE SAID/SHE SAID	SUPERVISORY COMMENTS
W: What movie are you watching?	
C: It's about Vikings, I don't know much about Vikings	
W: Me neither. So you like movies with war in them?	Assume
C: Yeah.	
(Start slow, maybe he doesn't want to speak.)	Closed question
W: So are you hot?	Closed question
C: No, I'm fine. It's cold outside.	
W: Yeah, it is really gloomy out today. Are you enjoying the MICA Meetings?	Topic change here
(Starting to sweat a little, maybe I should say you're sweating, but I think that would have put him deeper in his shell.)	So many topics: heat, weather, groups. Take a deep breath, slow down. I think your're sweating?

"The Rule of Three" applies to many situations in life. The first third of clients can sit down and express their needs and goals with little difficulty. They may change along the way, but basically they remain constant from start to finish. The second third have difficulty expressing their needs and they may change significantly before the end of treatment. What the first two groups have in common is that they have the capacity to express their needs. As you have already guessed, the last third of clients lack the capacity to identify their own needs and issues. This is where you, as their social worker, need to help your clients to identify their needs.

Client and student on first day:

HE SAID/SHE SAID	SUPERVISORY COMMENTS
W: Hi, I'm going to meet with you every Tuesday at 1:00. Do you remember my name?	We discussed, don't put the client on defense.
C: No.	
W: My name is. . . . Intro (Could've been better, I could have said I'm a student, I'm nervous.)	
C: What are we going to talk about?	

W: Anything you want to talk about, for example how your day is going.	Closed question, look for open-ended questions.
C: Good.	
W: How long have you been coming here?	Closed
C: A while.	
W: Do you enjoy it here?	Closed
C: Yes	

The student found herself with the problem of closed-ended questions. It is much easier to think of open-ended questions in the classroom with your peers than with a client. It takes time to feel relaxed so you can ask better questions. Part of the problem is not the questions, it is the responses. In conversations, we often ask closed-ended questions, but the person we are speaking with gives us more than a "yes" or "no."

With clients who can't express their needs and issues, you need to do two things: You need to feed them today; then you will be able to teach them to fish tomorrow to fend for themselves for much of their lives.

Whatever situation the client presents must be addressed, even if it truly seems unrelated to the client's goals and needs. So you must start with feeding the client where he or she is, and that may be far from where you think the client should be. But the client cannot move past the current situation until his or her initial concerns—however trivial or senseless they seem to be—are addressed in the session.

At this point, it really does not matter what you think is good for the client, because you don't know what the client's goals are yet. Think of how you can't really think about an upcoming test for Abnormal Psychology until you've eaten lunch. If you're starving, you will be internally distracted until you get your hunger taken care of.

> I was having so many problems at home that I could not concentrate on my internship. I was not sleeping well and was stressed all the time. I needed the family problems to get settled before I could really concentrate and hear what my supervisor was trying to teach me. Thank goodness, he understood and helped me by not moving too fast. I guess he was starting with me from where I was.

Now the second part becomes clear. You can begin to work on the issues and goals of the client once you have passed this hurdle, and teach the client to fish.

> A supervisor speaks: "I have a client in my private practice who has never made it past the need to be fed. Without going into all the dynamics of the case, this individual comes in always in need of being fed, at which point she does not come back for several weeks, until the next crisis in her life. Because of her style

of dealing with treatment, she has not learned to fish. Perhaps one day she will be able to move past this point, but until then the task of the social worker is to go at the pace the client sets.

Asking Open-Ended Questions

How many times have you been taught to ask open-ended questions instead of questions that can be answered with a one-word answer? Open-ended questions draw out clients and help them feel relaxed with you so they can "think out loud." Even though you have role-played countless times with your peers, when you begin your field work you may often find yourself in a situation where it feels like "pulling teeth" in order to get any useful information from clients. Thinking on your feet is a lot harder than practice situations, and it takes time to get the hang of it.

Student goes to dental school:

HE SAID/SHE SAID	SUPERVISORY COMMENTS
(Client is waiting to see me, I felt a little excited about today.)	
W: Do you know my name?	What made you ask this question?
C: No.	
W: My name is . . .	
C: Oh. (It's like pulling teeth!)	
W: So, did you have a nice weekend?	What do you know about the housing she lives in?
C: Yes.	
W: What did you do?	Good try, is she going to let you in?
C: Just sit . . . (. . . Searching for a lead-in question.)	
W: Just sit, did you go anywhere?	
C: No, just sit around.	
W: Did other people at the house go somewhere?	
C: No, they sat around.	

Leaving Space

Leaving space means that when you ask a question or make a statement, you leave enough time for the patient to reply to you. Leaving space may mean that you must learn more patience than you've ever had in your life. Although we are discussing the issue of leaving space here in the beginning phase, you will probably not fully understand the concept until you are well into the middle phase of your placement. Why is it so hard to leave space? Well, remember how anxious you are feeling as a student doing a first interview. There is a lot going on in the room and it takes time to develop these skills. You ask what you think is an open-ended question, and you are eager to hear your client's response. How eager are you? Did you leave time for the client to answer? When I say "enough time," I mean by the client's clock, not yours.

Leaving space allows time for your client to open up to you and respond. It has to do with your being able to tolerate silence and lack of immediate response on the part of your client. It seems so simple, and it looks like such a basic idea that you may think you should be able to leave space right from the beginning of your field work. You should know that leaving space is more difficult than it appears, and it has a great deal to do with your maturing skills. Don't get discouraged if you aren't able to master this skill immediately, because it takes time and experience. With this skill you will suddenly realize you are not as anxious and can concentrate on learning more of the skills and techniques of being with your clients in an effective way. A student who realized she had finally learned how to "leave space" once said, "I did not feel rushed and I was not hurried to ask the next question." She realized that she was able to elicit a response with the same question she asked on day one, but with the difference that now she was able to hear the response more fully and get an answer that led her to ask new questions.

Becoming the Least Motivated Person in the Room

Remember that your clients' goals are more important than your goals for them. You may have a hidden or overt agenda for your client, and believe that person should accomplish a particular result on a particular timetable. You must remember, however, that your world is not your client's world, and what is important is for you to support your client in making healthy choices (even though they may not be in line with your values or expectations). You must realize that clients have their own internal clocks, which may not coincide with your sense of time.

When I was younger, I expected clients to have certain goals. I expected them to be taking orderly and logical steps to achieve them and I expected them to take a minimum amount of time to get there. I wanted them all to have jobs, their own apartments, and good social skills. Imagine my frustration when my clients did not want the same things for themselves that I wanted for them. I was especially baffled when they seemed satisfied with lesser goals or were able to achieve goals by skipping steps I considered essential.

Asking

A very common error students make in the first days of their placement is to
assume they know what the client is meaning or feeling. You make these as-
sumptions based on your own set of values, not your client's. You may guess
correctly if the client shares your values, but too often you can guess wrongly
and then you are not helping your clients achieve their goals. In some ways,
you are clueless about what your clients mean in their statements. These as-
sumptions may leave clients feeling that their meeting with you was useless,
not helpful, or even destructive. Remember our earlier discussion on cultural
diversity when you find yourself assuming things rather than asking questions for clarity.

Learning to Tolerate Ambiguity and Ambivalence

As you are thrown into new situations and environments, you will find your
inner world enlarging. At times, you may be overwhelmed or confused about
all the contradictory data presented to you. You may find that you see some
of your most cherished beliefs in a whole new light in view of what you are
learning. You may find that at one point X seems to be true, yet at other times,
Y is also equally true even though they are totally opposite. You will find that
you do not have all the answers and that you may need to unlearn some of
your ideas. As a result, field placement may be a stressful and difficult time
as you adjust to seeing the world in new ways.

If you are committed to never opening your mind to new possibilities
or to never changing your ideas about something, you may be resisting new
ideas. It can be difficult to deal with inner conflicts, but, as you mature, you
will learn to be more tolerant of the clash of opposing ideas without trying to
oversimplify things so much that there is no more ambiguity.

As you mature as a social worker, you will also become more comfortable with your own ambivalence, as well as ambivalence in your clients'
thinking. We can have conflicting feelings about a given issue. You may love
someone dearly, yet have feelings of irritation and upset when there are conflicts. As you learn to accept your own divided emotions, you will be better
able to tolerate the inner conflicts of the clients in your placement.

One of my clients was in a long-term relationship with an abusive
boyfriend. She kept saying she was going to leave him, but at the same time
she really loved him and didn't want to live without him. I had worked with
her for several weeks, and was beginning to get very frustrated with her because she couldn't make up her mind and take the "right" actions. As I
processed my feelings with my supervisor, she explained to me that my
client was "sitting in the question," and was working through her ambivalence in her own way and in her own time. She also helped me to understand that my efforts to push her into what I thought she should do were

not helpful. In fact, I began to understand that by pushing in one direction, I was actually drawing out an opposite reaction in my client, and that was counterproductive.

Learning to Trust and Use Your Feelings

Before you can trust or use your feelings in working with clients, you must first be aware of what your feelings are. It may seem strange to state that you may not know what you are feeling in a particular situation, but if you are honest with yourself, you will admit that there are often levels of emotions that you were not aware of until you took time to delve deeper.

There are several ways to become more sensitive to your own emotions. You may want to write down various thoughts and feelings throughout your field placement. Journaling is one of the most important tools you can use to further your growth as a social worker. Your journal can serve as a log to jog your memory about dates or incidents, a record of the concepts and skills you have learned, and your growing maturity as a human being. The more honest you can be in your journal about your mistakes and shortcomings, the more the journal can teach you about yourself and how you can interact effectively with your clients.

Fortunately, the profession of social work enhances and encourages your ability to become a fully functioning human. As you encounter people who are different from and similar to you, you will be given more and more insight into your own behavior and emotions. You can also learn from the most negative of contacts with others, whether as clients or coworkers.

As you become more aware of your own feelings and insights, you will want to check your perceptions with others to see how accurate those perceptions are. When you "get a feeling" or hunch about something, it will be helpful to see to what extent others share your insights. Just because someone more experienced disagrees with you, however, doesn't mean that that person is right and you are wrong. You will benefit from an increasing openness in testing your reality with others. Over time, and with experience, you will naturally come to know that your feelings can be trusted.

Paying Attention to Your Body

As you learn to read your own emotions and bodily states, you will find that they are an enormous help in dealing with your clients. Listen to what your "gut" tells you. Does your stomach tighten up around certain people? Do you find you breathe more shallowly in some situations? What happens to your jaw muscles, your shoulders, your back? Where in your body do you tend to experience the emotions elicited in you by others?

For example, you may find yourself consistently getting angry or anxious with a particular client. Or you may find that you are suddenly sleepy and tired when dealing with another. The feelings elicited by clients can be important clues in understanding their behavior. You may want to think about the strong possibility that the client often brings about the same feelings in others in his or her environment. If a client is often making the people in his life angry, then his experience of the world will be different from that of a client who does not elicit anger in others.

> I was assigned to work with a policeman at our agency. The problems he was discussing were not anything I hadn't encountered with other clients. Yet, at every meeting, I found myself feeling anxious, and at times it was hard for me to concentrate on what he was saying. Clearly, he did not have the full benefit of my skills. In mentally searching for the reason why I was distracted, I realized he always came in civilian clothes, but he wore an off-duty weapon at his waist, not uncommon for police personnel. Having identified the source of my anxiety, I asked him if he could not wear the weapon to the office. He willingly left his weapon somewhere else, and then I was able to devote my full attention to his issues.

To trust and use your feelings:
  Believe that your feelings can help guide you
  Ask open-ended questions
  Breathe deeply
  Relax
  Start where the client is
  Build on your clients' strengths and support them
  Fous on your own strengths and on what you do well

CARE AND FEEDING OF ON-SITE SUPERVISORS

If you are lucky, your on-site supervisor will fulfill two important roles: He or she will teach you to become a great social worker, and become the kind of person you can look up to both personally and professionally. Ideally, your field work supervisor will also be your mentor. A mentor is often thought of as a more experienced person, a wise and loyal advisor. Mentors use their seniority to act as sponsor, host, guide, and example. Ideally, they serve as a role model, and offer guidance, support, and coaching in order to help students become successful. If you are very fortunate, you will have just such a supervisor. You can also increase the chances of bringing out the best in your on-site supervisor by the way you set the stage for your association.

Make it easy for the supervisor to deal with you. Set an emotional climate in which the supervisor feels comfortable with you and your level of cooperation. In the first few days, your supervisor will mentally breathe a sigh of relief when it becomes obvious that you're not a "problem student" and that you will be easy to work with.

Ask questions to gain knowledge, not to show off to a supervisor or others.

Let the supervisor know you're teachable and humble. One of the best ways to establish this humility is to admit honestly at the beginning that you're feeling anxious and unsure in your new role. Don't try to cover up your feelings of insecurity with false bravado. Mature students: This is not the time to demonstrate your ability to disguise your anxiousness.

Be a student. Be teachable, no matter how old or experienced you are.

Remember that you are undergoing two inherently regressive experiences: being in field work and being under supervision. That is, you will suddenly be thrust into the role of "newbie," in which you are automatically unsure of yourself and feel smaller and younger than before. That's par for the course. The fact that you have those feelings means that you fully understand what is happening to you. That's all. Feeling weak, small, incompetent, or uncertain is actually a positive step in the learning process, and those feelings (if honestly faced and dealt with) can help you learn, grow, and work well with others.

"In the beginner's mind there are many possibilities. In the expert's mind, there are few." Strive to cultivate beginner's mind so you can keep learning from the situations in which you find yourself.

You may have been taught to see supervisors as wise and all-knowing. For you to see your supervisor falter or do something that would negatively affect you or your performance may be unthinkable. But guess what? Your supervisors are human and they do make mistakes. Are they big enough to admit they made a mistake? That may depend on two factors: (1) the supervisor's maturity level, ability to self-evaluate, and level of psychological security, and (2) your ability to create an atmosphere in which a supervisor feels comfortable enough to say, "I made a mistake."

"That's not my job," you may say. "It is the job of the supervisor to make me comfortable enough to admit my own mistakes." You are correct. That is the supervisor's job. However, if you want to make your field placement more pleasant, meaningful, and productive, you will begin to think about the atmosphere you create for everyone around you—clients, staff members, and supervisors alike. A supervisor who feels comfortable with you can then relax and help make you feel relaxed, so it is a circular reaction. When you create that "safe zone" for another, you will be more likely to receive emotional safety in return.

We have all heard stories about students in tears after supervision, about supervisors not available to supervise, and about supervisors leaving mid-year for an assortment of reasons. As just mentioned, supervisory skill can vary and in some situations the supervisor may have been appointed unwillingly. These factors can greatly affect your placement; in these situations get the support of your college field work faculty, for they can guide you.

> Field work faculty have years of experience. They are an important resource.

How do you create an atmosphere of safety for your supervisor? Watch how others behave who deal well with your supervisor. Learn when and how to talk with your supervisor. An old saying reminds us that, because we have two ears and only one mouth, we should do more listening than talking. Talking in the context of deep listening is more powerful and more likely to be heard. Learn to "lead into" a topic after warm small talk and "setting the stage" with pleasant conversation instead of barging in and requesting something "cold." When you're requesting (not demanding) something or need to discuss something difficult, learn the best times to discuss (and not to discuss) uncomfortable subjects.

Not-so-good times to talk with your supervisor are:

- just after either of you have had a difficult encounter with a staff member or client
- during or after a tense meeting
- days that are unusually rushed and filled with tension
- whenever you detect signs of stress in your supervisor
- when you see your supervisor preoccupied with a concern or problem
- the end of the work day when everyone is tired
- just before or after a holiday
- any time you yourself are tired, angry, hungry, upset, or overly emotional

With that list there never seems to be a good time to meet with your supervisor, or so it would seem. Welcome to agency life; any or all of these things can occur in a given day. Learn to wait. Unless you're truly in an emergency situation, whatever you need to discuss with your supervisor will wait for later. Use your structured supervision time, write down the items you want to discuss, prioritize them. You may not get to everything on your agenda. Giving an issue more time and consideration will likely only help the situation. Make immediate notes so you won't forget what needs to be talked about. When you are angry, it is probably best to wait until you have processed the anger on your own, if you can. You might do this through introspection, calming down, journaling, talking to someone in your support group, walking around the block, if need be, or taking other measures to reach greater perspective and insight on your own. Again, your supervisor and field faculty are resources; if you are unable to process your feelings seek their assistance, and try to be open to what you hear.

Sometimes your supervisor may inadvertently give you unclear directions or bad advice. Calling attention to the situation, heckling, or laughing at a supervisor doesn't help. Ideally, the supervisor will realize what happened and will make every effort to correct the situation and acknowledge the mistake. A supervisor speaks:

> I was going to be off for the next few days, and I was unhappy with the progress note the student had written on a client. Because I was not going to be available, I asked a fellow social worker to speak to the student to help her understand what should be in the note and what should not be included. What a major blunder I made as a supervisor! The student did what the other social worked asked, but that person did not have a clear understanding of the background of the situation or the issues we were working on. As a result, the advice he gave her was directly contradictory to my supervision and what I had discussed for the last several weeks. No wonder she was confused!

Supervisors vary widely in their availability. Some supervisors are hard to find, have little time to talk, teach, or explain. Others may feel so pressured by various factors in their personal or professional environment that they are unable to give you the time and attention you may want or need.

Supervisors also vary in their ability to teach. You may run into the kind of supervisor who does very little teaching or explaining, and expects you to function on your own and learn from your own mistakes. "Just go out there and wing it, and if you run into problems, come find me and I'll help you out," you might hear. As luck would have it, when you do need that supervisor, he or she may be nowhere to be found, and you are left with a sticky situation that you do not know how to handle on your own. That's a time when you need support from others, whether it's a trusted friend, a school mentor, or a support group of your peers.

To get the most from the time you spend with your supervisor, bring your written agenda to each meeting. Keep the list with you at all times, so when something comes to mind, make a note of it for future reference. At the meeting, you will be able to keep discussion focused on the issues that are important to you, and you will not walk out of the meeting saying to yourself, "Oh, I forgot to bring up. . . ." This also shows your supervisor that you are prepared for the session. Everything you do is being evaluated, especially your attitude toward the work. Your professionalism is developing through this field placement experience and part of that experience is your behavior and attitude at meetings.

Over the years, I have been exposed to many supervisors, both good and bad. No matter how experienced supervisors are, they can still make mistakes. What I have learned is that even the poor supervisors have taught me lessons I have incorporated into my own style of working with clients..

NOTES TO YOURSELF

Reminders of things to do: _____
_____
_____
_____
_____
_____
_____
_____

Situations that relate to readings: _____
_____
_____
_____
_____
_____
_____
_____

Questions to ask your supervisor: _____
_____
_____
_____
_____
_____
_____
_____

Supervisor's comments: _____
_____
_____
_____
_____
_____
_____
_____

■ ■ ■ ■ ■ ━━━━━━━━━━━━━━━━━━━━━━━━━━━━━━━━━━━━━

CHAPTER 5

NAVIGATING THE HAZARDS

STRESS AND ANXIETY

If you didn't experience tension, stress, and anxiety while beginning a new field placement, you might have underestimated the magnitude of change you were about to experience. It is entirely normal to experience a certain amount of disorientation, confusion, and lack of confidence as you settle into your internship. Any new situation is bound to stir up old feelings you didn't remember you had, and, in particular, beginning field placement is an important change for you because it is a big step in preparing for what may be a life-long career. You must successfully pass through the "test" of field placement in order to move to the next level in your preparation.

You may be more stressed than you think. One of the difficulties with stress is the way it can sneak up on you and hit you just when you think you're coping well. If you're in doubt, or just for fun, you might investigate some ways of assessing the level of stress in your life. There is no one way to accurately measure the amount of stress in a person's life. There are many rating scales you can use to measure the amount of stress you are experiencing. While you may find it hard to devote the time to the task, it is well worth the effort. Your agency placement may use some of these scales and they may be available to you. The key element here is recognizing stressful situations you are exposed to at the time you are in placement.

On top of the usual and expected stresses of beginning a new situation, you may have additional stressors that have an effect on you. You may have family responsibilities or problems, financial concerns, health challenges, or you may simply have overscheduled your life with too many responsibilities, jobs, classes, or activities. No matter what your personal situation or what life problems you may be struggling with, you will be expected to keep those problems from affecting your work. When you walk through the door to your placement, your supervisor, your coworkers, and your clients all expect you to "tend to business" and be fully present instead of worrying about other things.

When your mind is taken up with personal problems, two things can happen. First, your mind may distract you so that you don't think things through fully; you may not understand a situation as well as you ordinarily would; and you may not be able to concentrate fully or make good contact with your clients. Your stressed state can cause you to make mistakes you wouldn't normally make.

Second, if you are very stressed, you may need to miss work in order to take care of emergency situations or your health. Everyone has a crisis or emergency occasionally, but it should not become a regular occurrence. Repeatedly missing days because of personal problems could seriously compromise your work/grade/progress. You need to demonstrate your dependability and maturity in taking care of your life outside your placement. This is part of learning to be a professional.

If you find yourself with an increasing amount of stress and anxiety, work now to prevent problems later. Take a good look at your calendar to see how you spend your time. Have you overscheduled yourself? What needs to change? What do you need to do differently? Whom do you need to ask for help? What changes do you need to make in your personal routines and habits?

Staying organized and planning ahead can prevent many problems later. Lay out your schedule in advance. Block in time for yourself and for rest and recreation. Highlight any papers or reports you must complete and give yourself your own personal deadline before the actual deadline to make sure you can meet your obligations with ease. Begin working on major projects far in advance. Pay particular attention to your daily schedule at your placement so you can show up on time for meetings and appointments. If you don't already have and use a day planner, start now. Make sure your transportation is reliable, and do whatever you need to do in advance in order to ensure that you get to work on time.

"A stitch in time saves nine," goes an old folk saying. Take care of tiny problems before they grow into big ones. Don't neglect important details.

Procrastination can become a major source of unnecessary stress. If you've made a habit of putting things off until the last minute, then rushing to complete them, you may find that, with your new responsibilities, such a pattern will no longer work for you. If you have a problem with delaying tasks and distracting yourself, start now to change your habits.

If you have had trouble getting yourself to class or work on time, make things easier for yourself. You may want to lay out your clothes for the next day, and make notes to yourself about tasks that need to be completed so you can get where you're going on time. You can make being on time a conscious decision. Make it a priority to establish the habit of being where you are supposed to be on time.

One reason some students experience stress in their field work placement is that working with clients in a particular population may stir up old feelings and memories from the past. These reactions may indicate that you have further work to do in integrating your own life experiences. These are supervisory issues, so one of the first things you must do is report these feelings to your supervisor. He or she will discuss them with you and help you to gain perspective in establishing the appropriate therapeutic distance from your clients. If you become wrapped up in your clients' difficulties, you will not be able to give them the assistance they need. In the first weeks of her field work, one student wrote:

> I find myself thinking about my clients all the time—while I'm driving on the freeway, as I shop for groceries, even when I'm trying to get to sleep. I worry about them, wonder if they're using drugs again, if they're managing to stay out of trouble. I can't continue to live like this with an upset stomach all the time. I'm going to have to talk to my supervisor.

These feelings do not indicate that you are not ready for field placement or that you are unsuited to social work practice. Such difficulties with separating your own life are a supervisory issue. Your supervisor has been able to help many students with this same issue because it is a predictable stage in learning to develop healthy boundaries. In addition to turning to your supervisor, you may want to spend some time in introspection, journaling, or talking to a trusted peer or teacher. In some cases, an inability to separate work from home life may indicate areas in which you have old, unresolved issues. If, despite excellent supervision and peer support, you find you are still having difficulties in this area, you may seek assistance in counseling in order to maintain your balance.

Fortunately, the practice of social work gives us the ways and means to understand and deal with our own issues with ever-increasing insight. As you work with clients with various issues, you will be given numerous opportunities to strengthen your boundaries, maintain an appropriate therapeutic distance, and become a stronger individual.

Even experienced social workers sometimes get so caught up in the needs of their clients that they forget to take the time they need for themselves. This problem is rampant in the helping professions. Those who help others may so identify with them and feel their pain that they become enmeshed in others' problems and challenges and are unable to deal with their own issues.

> I recall a student working in an after-school program. She became overly involved with one of the students, and, despite her supervisor telling her not to, she went to the child's home for dinner and to discuss the parent–child

problems. Her inability to see her overinvolvement resulted in boundary issues; she lost her objectivity and now was in conflict with her supervisor.

You will hear advice like "Don't get overly involved" or "Don't take your work home with you." Easily said, but very hard to do. Keep yourself mentally healthy. Make sure you get enough play, whether that is shopping, gardening, sleeping late, or renting a movie. Some people call it taking a mental health day.

Sharing information is also great for lowering your stress level. Sharing or just venting to a peer can be very soothing to the soul. Spend some time with your classmates and gripe about the work load, the teachers, your supervisors, and laugh a little.

Procrastination can be deadly. You need to stay on top of your work; that means structuring your time. Get a day planner. Put in time off to go out to dinner or to a friend's home. Scheduling play time will actually help you get more accomplished in the long run.

The higher your anxiety, the harder it is to "think on your feet." That's simple, right? The fact remains that thinking about your situation will help, but you need to share the burden of what is happening to you. Let your supervisor or a coworker know you are anxious. It will actually free you and lessen your anxiety because you have talked about it.

What happens when you become anxious? You look for mental structure. You've lived your life in structure and learned in structure even before you started school. You most definitely learned structure in early childhood from your family's eating and sleeping routines, along with the structure of kindergarten and early grade school.

Structure is a great thing. I am not criticizing it in any way. Structure, routines, and rituals make our lives easier and reduce our anxiety as we follow some kind of schedule, irregular though it may be. Structure makes life predictable. For example, you may have a morning ritual that works for you, such as drinking a cup of coffee, reading the morning newspaper, taking a shower, checking e-mail, and so on. Many people report that when their routines are disrupted they feel flustered, anxious, and "out of whack." The disruption creates unpredictability, which is what contributes to our stress.

It is clear that doing the same things in a certain order can be calming. But there is a negative side to order that needs to be addressed: with excessive anxiety, it is easy to fall into rigid thinking. Rigid thinking does not free you from the anxiety that you want to escape. Rigidity hinders you and you lose the ability to think clearly. As a result, you begin making errors in your sessions with clients and feel renewed anxiety over what to do, what to tell your supervisor. It is a vicious circle.

So, now that we have touched on the impact it will have on you, let us redirect our attention to the task of how to identify rigid thinking, both before you are in the session, when you feel stuck, as well as observing yourself "freezing up" in the session and out of the interview room.

Identifying your rigid thinking will require a critical perspective on your own actions and the ability to do self-analysis. The more anxious you feel, the more likely it is that you will retreat to a physical or emotional "safe zone" in which you can function by using excuses and phrases such as "She didn't understand," or "He's never worked in the field," or denial such as, "What is happening has nothing to do with me and my experience here, don't you agree?" Rigid thinking merely serves a defensive purpose: lowering your level of anxiety so that you feel more in control of yourself. A key concept to remember is that "freezing up" is not an effective tool, even though it might make you feel better for a short time. The freer you can be to do self-analysis, the faster you will be freed from the grip of rigid thinking. Even the acknowledgment that you suspect you have rigid thinking can free you up.

How you manage your stress levels is much more important than your own personal success in your internship. Remember that you serve as a role model, too. You want to be able to teach clients how to handle the major and minor hassles in their lives. One of the best ways to do that is by example. They will notice how you manage your own life and will learn by your example. This is an example of mirroring the behavior, as you will mirror behaviors of your supervisor.

YOUR INNER CLOCK

The inner clock of your clients may not keep time the same way as your clock, so you will need to learn how this affects your relationship to them. Often, seasoned social workers will come into supervision and report a situation in which they feel annoyed or angry with a client. This can easily be put under the topic of countertransference but it fits better under the general topic of skill building.

A visual illustration will help you understand. If I were to ask you and a client at the same time to stand and turn in a circle you would quickly see that the two of you would turn at different speeds. Only some of the time would you be face-to-face. You can try this with a friend to get the idea.

What this example shows is that people move at different rates. Such things as mental confusion due to stress, a traumatic event, or the effects of medication could all result in an individual moving now at a different rate than he or she usually would. Because of illness, trauma, medication, or various factors, his or her speed of thinking and moving may never again be the same for the rest of his or her life. We are always changed by the events in our lives, and some of them cannot be undone. Please remember this about your clients and be compassionate in your expectations of them.

The point is that you may forget the individual is a client and that may affect her or his ability to communicate with you. As you are feeling the anxiety of your newness to the profession, it is hard not to fill every silence and every gap in the conversation. Waiting for the client to process information and respond to you can feel like an eternity. Please understand that all you are doing is waiting until he or she turns and faces you, so to speak. There is an expression that "fools rush in where angels fear to tread," and so do social work students eager to help.

TRANSFERENCE AND COUNTERTRANSFERENCE

This is an easy topic to discuss when there are good examples; generally that means that someone is caught up in an issue. There are many articles and chapters of textbooks devoted to the topic of transference. To put it simply: Transference is something the client is feeling and/or acting on toward you, and countertransference is what you are feeling and/or acting on toward the client. What you learned in class is the theory of the concepts; they just feel differently when you are there in field work, "standing in the rain." Some examples from process recordings will illustrate typical situations.

Shocked student:

HE SAID/SHE SAID	SUPERVISORY COMMENTS
W: Looks like you have a lot on your mind.	
C: I just feel a lot of love in this room.	
W: OK. How are things at the residence?	
C: . . .	
W: . . .	
W: Is there anything you want to talk about?	Good question, but not the response you expected.
C: Yeah, I have feelings for you.	
W: Feelings for me? Silence	

Student handles situation:

HE SAID/SHE SAID	SUPERVISOR COMMENTS
C: What do you think about what I just said?	

W: You know that I am the social work intern and you are the client, right?	Good response
C: Yeah, but I feel like this love, like you care.	
W: Yeah, . . . I care for you, but as a social worker and client type situation.	Good
C: I know but I could no longer hold it inside of me.	Very open with you
W: Thank you for telling me how you feel.	Well done

First, let's discuss intent from the client's viewpoint. The client does not intend that you be a particular person as her or his mother or father. She or he is not using conscious thoughts in this process and saying to her- or himself, let's talk to this social worker as if she or he is one of my parents. Basically, transference is how the client interacts with the world and you are now part of her or his world. An example would be the client behaving in a certain manner with authority figures: You are an agent of the agency in your student role. So, while you are sitting there thinking how you are here to do good and rid the world of injustice, your client may be perceiving you in a very different way. Your task—and an important skill to learn—is to be yourself and not find yourself responding to your client based on how he or she wants you to respond.

An example of transference would be a client experiencing life situations as often rejecting her or him, perhaps by the tone of her or his voice or what he or she says. If you don't behave in the same rejecting way, he or she may try harder to get you to reject her or him. Your job as a social worker may require you to help clients see what in their manner leads people to reject them, and perhaps they may learn new skills at dealing with the world. Don't assume this task will be easy.

Human beings have long-established patterns of dealing with the world and we have perfected them, as dysfunctional as they may be: This is what we know how to do. Dealing with transference is an excellent example of why social work students have field placements: You cannot learn these skills in a classroom. We can only talk about transference to a point, then when it happens to you in the field, it is like a revelation, a "Wow, now I get it!"

Now, let's look at the second part, countertransference. You may say, "No, not me—I would never do that to a client." Really!? I have seen seasoned social workers as well as students dealing with countertransference issues; they are a part of doing social work.

At a meeting of social workers and psychologists discussing clients, one of the social workers with fifteen years experience began discussing one of her cases. As the others listened, they could hear a tone of anger in her voice. As she went on and on, she described a woman whom she had seen for many years who was currently asking for a new social worker, a request the social worker supported. As other members of the group asked questions, it became clear the client had always been friendly and happy, and had followed the social worker's recommendations. The client had recently gone to live in another state, a move not supported by the social worker. At the last visit, the social worker described the client as different: "angry and less cooperative." It seemed obvious to the rest of us that the social worker was angry with the client for leaving her and making the move to another state. The social worker very likely had some "baggage" to deal with, in this case unresolved abandonment issues.

This is one of the most common and obvious countertransference issues to see and experience. You must "start where the client is." This social worker forgot the golden rule: if she had seen the client's issues, having perhaps failure as an important issue, she would have addressed the patient's anger in a different way. Thank goodness clients so often give us a second chance to get it right.

More importantly for the long view, what do you do with this new information about yourself? We will discuss the need for self-evaluation in "When Things Go Bad." In this case, the social worker may have been correct in thinking the client made a bad decision. Nevertheless, the client still needed her help.

Remember that social work is about the client, not about the social worker. Save your self-righteousness for the locker-room; the client needs you to be professional. Learn from your mistakes and become a better social worker. If you are in a difficult situation and suddenly realize you are caught up in a countertransference issue, get help. Speak to your supervisor, be sure to do a process recording on this session, and write it in your journal to explore your own list of unresolved issues. In the case presented, the social worker was so entrenched in her feelings that she still insisted the client be transferred to another social worker. She needed to distance herself from the discussion to do some self-analysis and evaluation.

Sometimes, countertransference issues can sneak up on you. You may not have had the luxury to deal with the situation before. You may not have seen the problem developing. You may be unexpectedly confronted with these issues in supervision. In such a situation, you may feel "blindsided," hit by something that was there, but you didn't see it because of a blind spot.

Remember that our "baggage" and unresolved issues often create blind spots in our awareness. Try to remember: You are a student. You are in placement to learn. If you knew it all you would not have this field placement. Countertransference issues provide social workers (in training, fledgling, or highly experienced) with many opportunities for growth if we examine them and stop resisting or denying them.

I was out of the office one afternoon when a male student was confronted by his client, who suggested he had homosexual feelings toward the student. The student handled the situation well, but nevertheless, in the absence of a supervisor, he looked for a colleague to give him guidance and feedback for some unresolved fears. He realized that transference and countertransference were at work in the situation. The colleague he consulted gave the student an article to read on transference. He did need this information, but what he was really looking for was emotional support, which he didn't get. Learn to be patient and sit with your uncomfortable feelings. Wait until the right time to discuss what happened.

Tips: Read about transference and countertransference; get a basic understanding of the theory.

WHEN THINGS GO BAD

There will be times you will wish you had chosen another profession. It may come as a process recording that is being reviewed or at your semester evaluation. It is so easy to be in a situation where you suddenly begin to feel that everything is going wrong and you are a failure. What if your supervisor has already taken you to task on spelling and grammar, your self-esteem is wounded, and you actually begin to hate your supervisor? The feelings and situations can happen so fast. You need to be prepared for these times as best you can.

You may be the only one feeling that things are going wrong, and your supervisor may think things are fine, or the situation can be the reverse. How do you handle a situation that seems hopeless and requires you to rethink your entire life's mission? This is like preparing yourself for a worst possible scenario; your preparation can never be adequate to the real situation. On the other hand, you may want to ask yourself, "What's the worst possible thing that can happen?" and be prepared to handle it if and when it does.

First, you must remember you did not make it this far in social work on your looks. You are here because you were qualified and overcame all the hurdles to get to a placement. Second, your job is to learn as much as you can in the time you are in the placement. Those learning experiences may include a poor evaluation or the demise of a process recording. Third, you may have a great supervisor or a poor supervisor who is working out personal problems on you. Remember that transference and countertransference happen between you and your supervisor, too. Yes, that happens all the time and the school can only help you so much. Fourth, remember that everything is a learning experience, including having difficulties with your supervisor.

But let us address the concerns you may be having in your current situation, beginning with the parts of the problem: you, the supervisor, and your work. Now start to evaluate the problem from all directions; be honest in your evaluation, and if you can't be honest with yourself, ask a peer for input. If you ask for input from peers, don't lead them to agree with you, by the way you present the situation, so they can only validate your opinion. Give them the facts and see where they lead. The more honest you are with yourself, the clearer the picture. What are you doing? What are your issues or problems? What "emotional baggage" have you brought to the agency? Now think again! You know this stuff; you have been over it dozens of times with your college field advisor. The difference is that now you are facing the issues in real life, a "messier" business than dealing with theories on the printed page. This is all part of making the leap from theory to practice.

Supervisors are the same as classroom professors. Figure out what they want and give it to them. Easily said, but hard to do. Okay, make a list in the margin, right now. What "emotional baggage" have you brought with you that may be part of the problem or getting in your way? Have you had negative life experiences that make you fearful or less than objective in dealing with people and situations?

What are your supervisor's expectations? Now you will have two lists: your baggage and your supervisor's expectations. Look closely at both the lists. What are you leaving out? Now think of yourself as a consumer of services. After all, you have invested time and money to get this far in your career, and, in a sense, you are "buying" the services of field work to train you as a social worker. What are your goals? What steps are needed to get there?

You say you are meeting the supervisor's expectations: Can you prove it or show evidence that you are? Again, make a list of specific ways you have fulfilled those expectations. The situation may be as it is because you or your supervisor or both of you are not on track to meet the goals of your placement. What does your learning contract specify? Are you on target for reaching these goals? Why is it that you and your supervisor are not "on the same page"?

Your college faculty placement supervisor needs to be kept informed if you have difficulties with your placement. Remember, he or she is a resource.

An important lesson to learn: You are only as good a social worker as you are willing to evaluate your own work and continue to grow from your mistakes. It is your responsibility to evaluate clients' work. When a client stops coming in or misses an appointment, you need to look at the situation and ask "What happened?" Did I say something or not do something that caused this to happen? And what are my client's issues that may be part of the process? Use every situation to learn and grow. If there are things you should have done differently, own up to them and learn from them.

You can use your mistakes productively with your clients, expressing where you may have been wrong. Don't be afraid to apologize if you made a mistake. This will demonstrate to your clients your willingness to work with them, improving the relationship and the trust.

On the other hand, you need to learn that many clients (for a multitude of reasons) simply don't avail themselves of available services. They begin sessions, then end them abruptly for no apparent reason. Realize that a certain percentage of the people you are trying to help act as if they don't want or need you or the agency. With a wide and long experience base, your supervisor should be able to help you gain perspective on this persistent problem. Don't take it personally!

Remember that your relationship with your supervisor is a mirror or parallel of what you are doing with your clients. If you are having difficulties with your supervisor, your clients may be having problems with you.

Own your mistakes! They are your friends. They will help you grow.

Three Common Mistakes

There are three common mistakes that many students make in their field placements. We have given them pet names and stick-figure drawings so past students will always remember: "Drowning in content!" "Got you hook, line, and sinker!" and "The ship sailed without you on it!"

Drowning in Content.   Here we have a common problem of content, content, content and going nowhere. Lots of words, but no point. There are times when the client is a great talker and will chew your ear off, or a person who talks about nothing. This is the drowning part for the student; here you wish you could ask a closed-ended question so the person would "just shut up." Also, there are topics that often go nowhere, such as politics and religion. If you are drowning in content, you have to learn to redirect your client to a more useful or productive topic. Help him or her make a point.

Got You Hook, Line, and Sinker!   Often, a client will present you with a bogus topic to get you off track or deliberately mislead you. This may be done consciously or unconsciously, but the result is that you have been "reeled in." You have been taken in, "buffaloed," or manipulated by the client and you lose your train of thought and original purpose. Another phrase for this ploy is, *red herring,* an item meant to distract people and throw them off track. Learn to listen for a client introducing a new topic: Is it legitimate, or is it bait to reel you in? If it's bait and you bit on it, the original topic is gone.

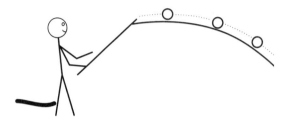

The Ship Sailed Without You On It.   This is my all-time favorite. This situation happens to every student I have had over the years. A client presents an important topic in the session (we may have even discussed the topic in supervision), but the student doesn't or can't hear it, perhaps because of a high anxiety level.

Uncomfortable Topics

Topics that make you squirm can come up on the first day you start your placement, or at any time you meet with clients. A client brings up a topic you find difficult to talk about, such as sex (whether to have it or not, how to avoid it), incest, abuse of self, victims of rape and violent crimes, death of significant persons, victims of child abuse, abortion. The list goes on and on. Many topics that can spark uncomfortable feelings in your client may be difficult for you as well.

Surprised Student:

HE SAID/SHE SAID	STUDENT FEELINGS
W: You have told me a lot about your father's family, now tell me a little about your mother's family.	
C: OK, well, it was kind of painful to live there. My father hit me with a wire.	Visible shift here—he was uncomfortable
W: Now old were you?	
C: Maybe about five or six.	Trauma assessment????
W: Did that happen often?	
C: No, not really. He chased me . . .	
W: Then what happened?	
C: My father left but they came and took my sister to foster care.	

This situation with the student's client was a complete surprise to her. Her questions may not have been open-ended all the time but she hung in there. The main thing here is that client's history: It is important in order to understand your client. Also, you can never tell where you will be led in the session.

Remember, there are two issues on the table: how the client feels and how you are feeling. Many students try to ignore their own uncomfortable feelings so the client will drop the issue to avoid these feelings in both client and student. That tactic works well some of the time to reduce anxiety in the short term, but, of course, you realize that if you shut your client down on that topic, you have lost a valuable opportunity to discuss significant issues and make long-term progress. Some clients are persistent and keep presenting the topic again and again in a different way, as if to say, "Hello, I have something to say to you." So, the ignoring-it approach will not get you the relief you want. You need to get past your own personal discomfort because sooner or later you will have to address these issues in your client meetings and with your supervisor.

Oh, how we dread the second! The client has brought this issue to the table. There can be a dozen reasons for you and your supervisor to ask: Why now? It does not matter. You have to deal with it. Use the skills you have at your disposal all the time: the ability to ask questions. Use your natural interest in the client to ask questions about the topic. A simple question like "What made you think of that issue?" or "Is this an important issue? Can you tell me more?" In some situations the topic introduced may be the result of a recent event that triggered the client's memory and the introduction of the topic.

> A client has just come from a health group where the topic was sexually transmitted diseases. The client now begins the meeting with, "I was thinking of joining the Marines, but I am not sure, because I will have to have a lot of sex when I am on leave."

It is up to you whether or not you try to shut down the topic just because it makes you uncertain or uneasy. As you learn to be an effective social worker, you will see how important it is for you to be able to deal with "sensitive topics" within your own experience. As you mature in your abilities, you will become more and more able to allow your clients to explore difficult subjects without emotional reactions or "running away" on your part.

The issue of trust is always there in the relationship. From the day you start with a client to the last time you are together—be it after six months or two days—you must establish trust with your client. Engagement may be the most important part of work with clients. If you have not established a working relationship built on trust, it is unlikely that your clients will bring up these topics unless they are testing your commitment to them.

HELPLESS AND HOPELESS: BAD FEELINGS OR GOOD FEELINGS?

Every social worker at some point in training will likely experience feelings of helplessness and hopelessness. This is a good place to be as a student, though at the moment it may not feel like a good place to be. These feelings are tremendous learning opportunities and, at the same time, give you insight into the feelings of your clients, as well as those of their family members or significant others.

Let's look at the feelings of helplessness and hopelessness and try to achieve a deeper understanding. As providers of services, we listen to situations in our clients' lives that cause them great discomfort. There is a natural feeling of wanting to do something to help, to lessen their emotional pain, that is more than just listening to the client. Often our clients will say to us, "Don't just sit there, say something." This statement evokes two reactions that you need to understand.

First, your need to help or do something may be driven simply by your discomfort with the feelings you are experiencing while with this individual. This is a common feeling that happens when you are working with clients. When the client says, "Say something," that doesn't mean you need to be her or his rescuer. Rescue mentality and behaviors are driven by your inability to tolerate discomfort. Your client may simply be asking for your empathy, compassion, and understanding.

If you are having these uncomfortable or helpless feelings while dealing with your client, remember that you may not be alone with these feelings. The family members and friends may have the same feelings when in the presence of your client. This may give you a clue as to why others do not want to have frequent contact with your client. These are not warm and fuzzy feelings, and what people try to do is come up with ideas to help, and at the same time lower the intensity of these feelings inside themselves; that is what you will want to do as well. But you will not, because you will talk to your supervisor before you act.

The key is to understand what you are doing for your client and what you may want to do for yourself. So why is it a good thing to feel these feelings? Because you get an understanding of what others may experience with this client and you can learn to use your feelings as a guide.

Second, interventions for the moment will not last. Clients need to find solutions that they can use when they are not with you, which is most of the time. That seems obvious, but when you are in there with the client, it is much harder to understand and remember. You often will get anxious because you feel you are not being helpful "enough" to your client.

You may have a hard time finding material to read on helplessness. At times you may get confused about where the line is in the sand that says "Now I give suggestions" and "Now I just listen." The difference is learned by practice in the field and by trial and error. Remember the difference between errors of technique and errors of the heart. If you made an intervention and it failed or went poorly, you don't make another one without some evaluation of the situation. Try not to make the same mistakes twice; clients are willing to give you a second chance. Watch your feelings and use them as a guide. If you are feeling helpless and hopeless, don't suggest quick fixes.

GIMMICKS AND PROPS

It seems like a contradiction to look for props to do your job in a profession that uses verbal skills. There are times and situations that require props, but that is not the general rule. There are times that sitting with your clients and doing genograms with them can really engage them in the moment, and there will be times you will be filling out forms with your clients.

> I was sitting in my office one morning doing some paperwork when my social work student arrived for the day. She was carrying a golf putter, golf balls, and a box containing a battery-operated putter cup. I was aware we had a new client in the program who enjoyed golf so I quickly put it together. When I asked, she gave a logical explanation for why she thought these props would be useful in establishing rapport with her client.

However, the student had not yet engaged the client in conversation, but had made the assumption that this game would be a way to relate to the client. It is likely that she was looking for a way to fill the time with her client. She lacked the confidence to rely on her verbal skills as a social worker. Remember to look at how you are feeling in the situation. Facing your feelings in such a situation can be difficult. You also need to deal with your general anxiety about placement, supervision, and lack of confidence, but the anxiety is essential to your learning.

A student came to me and said she had run out of ideas to help a client and wanted me to give her suggestions. I asked what she had been working on in the sessions; that's what supervisors ask. She responded that she had worked on getting the client in a program so he could get a high school diploma. What she failed to do was start where her client is! In this case the client had very low motivation and had difficulty just getting up and dressed in the morning, so the goal of a high school class was not realistic at this time. To work on this goal prematurely will set the client up for failure. The prop in this situation was the student's comfort in making calls to find out how to apply and filling out applications.

The following process recording is an example of using pamphlets as props. What you see is the well-planned intentions of the student.

HE SAID/SHE SAID	SUPERVISORY COMMENTS
C: I sleep a lot, this medication is making me tired.	
W: That is one of the side effects of . . .	
W: (I reached into my desk drawer, where I keep all the information pamphlets.) This doesn't tell a lot about all of the meds, but it does talk about . . . (I point out the side effects.) Would you like to keep this book?	Sense you are avoiding topics, why talk about medication, is that within your control? Why are you looking for material on his medication?
C: No, thank you.	

W: OK, well if you do want one,
there are more in the hallway.

C: I'm not sure if I am on . . .

W: . . . is for your illness.

Let's review the topic of using props: First, always start where the client is. Second, always start where the client is! Know what your client's needs are and you will always be moving in a positive direction. Keep a realistic view of what you and your client are working toward: In order to get to C you have to start at A and pass B. A client who wants to start at C may be headed for failure. Your job is to be there for your client. If your client wants to start at C, then, whether or not you approve, that is where the client is.

NOTES TO YOURSELF

Reminders of things to do: _____

_____

_____

_____

_____

_____

_____

_____

Situations that relate to readings: _____

_____

_____

_____

_____

_____

_____

_____

Questions to ask your supervisor: _____

_____

_____

_____

_____

_____

_____

_____

Supervisor's comments: _____

_____

_____

_____

_____

_____

_____

■ ■ ■ ■ ■ ▬▬▬▬▬▬▬▬▬▬▬▬▬▬▬▬▬▬▬

CHAPTER 6

TERMINATION

Ending is a complex subject. First, you are not just terminating with the agency and clients. You are also terminating with the staff at your placement, your college if you are a senior, fellow students, and the lifestyle of a student. This is a process that cannot be taken lightly, but its impact is often underestimated.

Be aware of all the terminations you are experiencing at the same time. It can evoke many feelings in you and the people around you, both staff and clients. No one can make the process less intense, but you can learn coping skills to deal with the changes and maximize the learning as you close out the field placement.

Endings can be an opportunity to reflect on the progress you have made in becoming a professional social worker. It is also a time to assess the progress your clients have made in their stay with you. Above all, termination is an evaluation period of your work. This is a real opportunity to reflect on your experience and evaluate your work as a professional social worker.

If you have not taken my advice to write in a journal over the course of the year, it is not too late. Writing may help you organize and understand the feelings you experience at this time.

CLIENT TERMINATION

I will start with termination with clients, as this can occur at any time while you are in your placement. Termination can occur for various reasons during the course of your placement. Agency life is not neat. It is not organized so that clients terminate with you at the same time you terminate from the agency. Some of the clients assigned to you may move on long before your time is up. Others will need to be transferred to other staff at your agency. Their treatments or goals may not be completed; however, you still will need to terminate with your clients.

Termination is a bridge that many of us would rather not take because it is often filled with feelings of loss and sadness. Ending a placement can even evoke unresolved feelings about past losses in your life. Some terminations will not bring with them strong feelings, but others will. The level of feelings evoked will depend on the nature of the time you spent with your clients and your level of engagement with them.

You must understand that termination may occur on many levels, so you need to stay alert to experience whatever is happening to you emotionally. There will be distraction at the end of the term, finals, and, if you are a senior, you will have graduation to think about. There is a great deal to learn in the termination phase, so stay focused.

Remember that termination affects your supervisor as well as you, the student. A supervisor speaks:

> I have to force myself to stay on track with my students as I begin to separate from them and experience the pending feelings. Deep down, I would rather ignore the termination process, and I am sure I could get many students to collude with me. Sad and angry memories can be awakened at these times, along with many other confused, ambivalent, and difficult feelings. This process is happening to the students, to me, and to the entire agency staff. We have all grown close. It's hard to say goodbye.

Clients are often experts at termination, having over the years had many social workers come and go. But were these terminations positive experiences, the type that you hope will help your client grow in relationships?

There are books written on the subject of termination, how to do it correctly and what it means to your client. In the end, you still have to say goodbye when you leave.

You may say that you would like to avoid termination by just going silently into the night. But guess what? You just did one type of termination. And after an extended time doing a placement you do have feelings about your clients and the people you spend the day with at the agency.

Here are some samples of process recordings dealing with termination. These are real-life examples, and should not be mistaken as the only or ideal way to terminate.

The first one describes a meeting with a client about three weeks before the end, meaning they may have about three more sessions together at most.

Student begins termination:

HE SAID/SHE SAID	SUPERVISOR'S COMMENTS
W: I've told you that I will be leaving at the beginning of May. (Remind him and prepare for our termination. I have to think of how I'm going to terminate.)	I know termination is being discussed in class but we have not discussed it.
	Feels like "Don't get too close—I am leaving."

C: Yeah, you're gonna make a great social worker.

W: Thank you.

C: Who can I talk to when you're gone?

W: Well, that's something I've been thinking about. You worked with . . . first, right?

C: Yeah, she was nice.

W: You liked her?

C: Yeah.

(I was relieved.)

I think you just terminated with the client.

Just because you are discussing termination in class does not mean it is time to start termination in your field work. Learn the standard in the agency where you are. Some supervisors like a month of preparation and lead time with the clients. Other agencies prefer a shorter time frame. There are no strict rules for this and you need to follow the policies of your agency, not your classroom professor or some author you read in class. If you find yourself in conflict, then you must put the issue on the table for discussion with both your field supervisor and the facility/placement supervisor of your college.

Be aware of your motivations. You're anxious to finish college and your field work, anxious to complete this final phase before you forget the material and get it done so you can focus on the papers you have put off starting until the last few weeks. The closer you get to the end of the year, the harder it can be to concentrate. You need to be aware of what you are feeling and how those feelings affect your work. If you are fortunate and have a good supervisor, he or she will help you stay focused on the topic of termination and separation from the agency. As stated before, be aware of your feelings in each session with your client. This is a valued tool for the client–social worker process.

How have the clients expressed concern about who will help them when you are gone? The student had been thinking about this and was ready with an answer. In this case she knew the agency policy was that clients that were given to students returned to their prior social worker. But what if she had not discussed the transfer with the previous social worker or with her supervisor? You can see the importance of having discussed this with your supervisor before the topic is discussed openly and before commitments are made.

Remember that rule in the chapter on ethics: Always be honest and truthful to your clients. In this case the student was very honest, but another issue was not addressed. The client said he liked the previous social worker, but the student assumed the client meant that she was a good person to talk to about his issues, but it could mean something else. It might mean, for example, that he found her attractive. It is better to explore and ask than to assume.

In this case, starting termination met the need of the student, as she was anxious to start termination and reassure her client he would be seen. His liking the previous social worker reassured the student. You can see that there are several issues in this situation. The student was discussing termination in class and was eager to start the process. The student wanted to assure the future of her client, of whom she was now feeling protective after a school year together. Simply put, she wanted to do a good job. I hope this very simple example helps you see some of the complexity of termination work.

> Students often worry about being good students and always doing the right thing, whether for the client or for their supervisor.

There are no set rules as to how to terminate with a client. There are guides and each agency has its own views on the topic, as there are different views among workers at the agency. In many agencies, the client population has experienced more terminations than you have. They have seen social workers, psychiatrists, case managers, intake workers, and assorted other professionals come and go. The clients may be very connected to the agency or institution. These kinds of clients have a wealth of experience with both good and bad terminations with staff.

The next process recording was made close to the time the student would be ending with the client; it demonstrates there is work until the very end.

HE SAID/SHE SAID	STUDENT'S FEELINGS
C: . . . I haven't seen my child in five years. She is nine now.	She seems very confused today. I will check with her residence to see what her counselor thinks.
W: She's an adult now and you have a grandson.	
C: Yes, I know.	Still thinks that her daughter is a small child.
W: I have not been able to reach her.	
C: No? I want to speak to her. I love my children.	
W: I am trying to find her but I am leaving in two weeks.	
C: You're leaving? Where are you going?	We discussed this last week.

W: . . . will take my place. She
will meet with you.

C: I will miss you.   I feel I really made a connection with her.

W: Thank you, I will miss you, . . .
will take good care of you.

C: Yes, thank you, can I go now?   I wonder if she is avoiding the
                                             termination topic here.

As you can see, this termination was different, but there were still issues. I want to point out that we tend to block out topics that are unpleasant to us, like termination. So I tell my students don't be surprised when a client says, "You never told me you were leaving!" With that point in mind remember this: Don't discuss termination in the fourth week before the end and then not mention it the next time you are with the client. I realize you, too, would like to avoid the topic, but your job is to help the client deal with your leaving. In this example, you can see that the student must have spoken about leaving in an earlier session because the client begins to talk about the loss of the children and wanting to see them.

Many times the topic of termination will come up in a discussion that involves a loss that may seem unrelated at first. The loss may include anything from a pet cat or dog, aquarium fish, lost objects, or people from the past who are missed. You may not pick this up when face-to-face with your client, and may only become aware after the fact, but you then can use it in the next meeting. It can be easier to spot this topic in a group because they are often co-led, so you are not constantly "on;" while others in the group address each other, you may have time to spot such a substitution.

Your supervisor will be a good source to discuss how termination topics are discussed in that particular agency and the norm for their population. That does not mean you should assume that all terminations in that agency are the same or alike. What is important to learn is the process of termination. How it is done in your placement may not be the same in other agencies. Ask your supervisor specific questions:

- What is the agency's policy on termination?
- What is the time frame your supervisor suggests?
- What are the usual pitfalls of the termination process?

EVALUATION AND TERMINATION

This is a time to reflect on where you began with the client and where you are now. You have probably heard students say they did not accomplish what they had set out to do with a client. A frequent pitfall is: Whose goals are we talking about? We know that you want your clients to reach their maximum potentials, but they will often fall short of your goals for them. Stay focused and remember it is their life, their progress, and their goals, not yours.

Remain as positive as you can during this phase. Spend some time reviewing your client's history with you, look at your notes, process recordings, and speak to your supervisor. You may be surprised to find there has been movement where you did not originally detect it. Then, while discussing endings with your clients, be reflective: Ask them how they see where you two began and where you both are now. See what they think is significant and, if you did your homework, you are prepared to interject the points of change and progress you have seen.

TERMINATION AND CLOSURE
AFTER THE CLIENT HAS LEFT

There are times when your client will have left and there will not be time to process the termination. There can be many reasons for this to occur in agency life. Clients may move, get or lose jobs, have major life changes, or have other reasons for leaving. At times, clients may say to you that they wish to terminate with you. They may or may not give you a reason. I could make a long list of reasons for this, from the client being mandated to a service, to other staff at an agency not letting go of the patients for various reasons. Remember not to take it personally when a client decides to terminate with you and/or the agency.

If you can, explore with them the reasons they feel they want to end. It is also an opportunity to discuss the progress of treatment and the benefits of continuing. Too often clients are overpowered by your status (after all we know what is best, right?) and agree to continue, but in their heart they want to stop. So they cancel appointments, come late, are "no shows," and at some point feel they are not getting anything out of your sessions and quit.

Now you have two tasks: explaining to your supervisor what happened and writing a discharge note or summary. This is not a bad thing to happen. You are the student, and you are not expected to know everything, and this can be an important learning experience. Once again you need to reflect on your work with the client, looking at the progress and events that led you to this moment. This is very important work, and you will not always have a supervisor to guide you. Critical analysis of your work is to be treasured.

Reflective thinking is a critical skill of a professional social worker. Not all social workers are equally skilled at this task and it does require a willingness to explore the possibility that you contributed to the client's decision. Being a professional means taking ownership even if it is not favorable. I can not teach you or refer you to a book that will teach you to be reflective in your professional social work practice, but I can tell you that good supervision, supportive peers, and a willingness to be open will help you develop this important skill.

YOUR TERMINATION

This is an important step that often is not fully understood, perhaps because of the strong emotions involved. In *The Practicum Companion for Social Work* (2000), Berg-Weger and Birkenmaier have put together a nice list of questions to ask yourself, so it is well worth the time to read over this list and others they provide in their text. Often, in social work department offices you will find a small library of textbooks. This is a time when students often reflect on their social work internship and ask themselves:

- As a social worker, am I good enough?
- Do I like what I am doing?
- Is there a place for me in the field? Where is my niche?

You have experienced learning in the micro, mezzo, and macro levels of social work practice in your placement. The micro level has been addressed with client termination and varying amounts of direct client contact. But no placement is without also negotiating mezzo and macro levels. Often, because of the intensity of placement work and the enormous amount of time and emotional energy that goes into a placement, it's hard to see the forest for the trees. If your placement was focused on direct care, your experiences of the mezzo and macro level may be less obvious to you. At times you may have been in a situation that required you to help your client negotiate the system. But there are many levels to your placement that need to be mentioned. As I discuss the client and the three levels of practice, there is also you, the student, and the three levels of your internship. As I discuss in mirror-mirror, what happens to you in your placement in an agency with supervision is happening to your client at the next level. You may not see this clearly till the placement is over and you are in a different place. Or you may come face-to-face with this process in the end stages of your placement. Whenever it happens, it is a time for you to learn at a different level than you have up to that point. I do not wish to sound vague or too philosophical, but this, like transference and countertransference, you need to experience to fully understand. These are areas that will appear on your end-of-the-year evaluation, perhaps not stated this way but ever present. Your understanding of this complex picture on multiple levels is an example of your becoming a professional social worker.

Here are just a few questions to get you started thinking about your placement and the role you played. Often social work students feel powerless and do not recognize the impact they have on their clients, and on the agency as well. Students do have an effect on the agency where they do their placement and, perhaps, on their college. Students placed at our agency are asked to do an organizational change project as part of their social work college curriculum, and several of those projects have been used over time.

For example, one student suggested we have an educational health component in the agency. She approached the nurse, who then ran a health group, and was able to effect change in the agency that lasts to this day. It was a small action that produced big rewards. Many of our clients do not eat breakfast, so she introduced a fruit bowl placed near the sign-in sheet. Sounds simple, yes, but the gains were great.

MIRROR-MIRROR

This topic has been mentioned a few times in this book. It is presented here again because you will have the greatest opportunity to understand this experience while you are reflecting on your placement.

Your experiences with your supervisor are often a reflection of the work you are doing with clients assigned to you. As you prepare to terminate with your clients, your supervisor is preparing to terminate with you. As you have been reflective with your clients and reviewed their progress, your supervisor will review your progress. You have looked at the notes you have taken on your clients, the process recordings, and any contracts/goals you and your client agreed to work toward. You have a learning contract that you set out to meet that you and your supervisor agreed on. This is an opportunity to reflect on your progress in your placement. Do not be surprised if you find that you have quickly met some of your goals, some were never addressed after doing the learning contract, and there were other learning goals that you experienced and never knew you had. This experience may be very similar to the experiences of your clients. This is an example of the mirror-mirror concept. I have touched on this topic in my discussion of the many levels of learning.

Once again, this is part of becoming a professional social worker. The more time you are exposed to the field in your placements and in your future work, the more you will begin to recognize this phenomenon. So, what is mirror-mirror exactly? Well, you can call it a parallel process or parallel processes. You can think of it as being in a fish bowl with your client and you, your supervisor, and the agency on the next level of the fish bowl. Or, you can see the process as simply a reflection. How you conceptualize this process is not as important as your understanding of the phenomenon.

NOTES TO YOURSELF

Reminders of things to do: _____

_____

_____

_____

_____

_____

_____

_____

Situations that relate to readings: _____

_____

_____

_____

_____

_____

_____

_____

Questions to ask your supervisor: _____

_____

_____

_____

_____

_____

_____

_____

Supervisor's comments: _____

_____

_____

_____

_____

_____

_____

SUGGESTED READINGS

Berg-Werger, Marla, and Birkenmaier, Julie (2000). *The Practicum Companion for Social Work.* Allyn and Bacon, Boston, MA.

Covey, Stephen R. (1990). *The 7 Habits of Highly Effective People, Powerful Lessons in Personal Change.* Simon and Schuster, NY.

Hamilton, Gordon (1951). *Theory and Practice of Social Case Work,* 2nd edition. Columbia University Press: NY.

Hollis, Florence (1972). Casework, *A Psychosocial Therapy,* 2nd edition. Random House, NY.

Horejsi, Charles R., and Garthwait, Cynthia L. (1999). *The Social Work Practicum, A Guide and Workbook for Students.* Allyn and Bacon, Boston, MA.

Johnson, Louise C., and Yanca, Stephen J. (1998). *Social Work Practice: A Generalist Approach.* Allyn and Bacon, Boston, MA.

Kadushin, Alferd (1972). *The Social Work Interview.* Columbia Press, NY.

Kirst-Ashman, Karen, and Hull, Jr., Grafton H. (2002). *Understanding Generalist Practice,* 3rd edition. Brooks and Cole, Pacific Grove, CA.

Lukas, Susan (1993). *Where to Start And What To Ask, An Assessment Handbook.* W.W. Norton: NY, NY.

Pincus, Allen, and Minahan, Anne (1973). *Social Work Practice, "Model and Method."* Peacock Publishers, Inc.: Itasca, IL.

Prochaska, James O., Norcross, John C., and Diclemente, Carlo C. (1994). *Change for Good. A Revolutionary Six-Stage Program for Overcoming Bad Habits and Moving Your Life Positively Forward.* Avon Books, NY.

Sands, Roberta G. (2001). *Clinical Social Work Practice in Behavioral Mental Health, A Postmodern Approach to Practice with Adults.* Allyn and Bacon: Boston, MA.

Sevel, Judith; Cummins, Linda, and Madrigal, Cesar (1999). *Social Work Skills Demonstrated.* Allyn and Bacon: Boston, MA.

Shi, Leiyu, and Singh, Douglas A. (1979). *Delivering Health Care in America. A Systems Approach,* 2nd edition. Aspen Publications: Gaithersburg, Maryland.

Shulman, Lawrence (1979). *The Skills of Helping Individuals and Groups.* Peacock Publishers, Inc.: Itasca, IL.

Slater, Lauren (1996). *Welcome To My Country: A Therapist's Memoir of Madness.* Random House, NY.